AF189959

As Above, So Below

My Life as an Adept

An Autobiography

by
Seila Orienta

Cover design by Peter Windsheimer.

Original German Title: Das Leben und die Erfahrungen eines wahren Hermetikers.

Translated into English by Peter Windsheimer.

Additional material by Peter Windsheimer.

Disclaimer
The author and publisher of this material are not responsible for injury that might occur, physically, emotionally or mentally, through misuse of the exercises and instructions contained within this publication.

Copyright© 2015 by Peter Windsheimer,
Boca Raton, Florida; USA.

Production and Publisher
BoD – Books on Demand, Norderstedt
ISBN: 9783744819121

All rights reserved. No part of this publication may be reproduced, stored in a retrieval system or transmitted in any form, electronic, mechanical, photocopying or recording in any form.

Table of Contents

BOOK II

Foreword

As the oldest son of Seila Orienta, I wholeheartedly corroborate all that my father has written in this book is based on true experience and is the truth.

Often, a lack of recognition and acknowledgement of the deeds of great spirits seems to be a fate that these masters share. I am certain that some readers will ridicule and discredit all that my father had and still has to offer. Even some of Seila Orienta's students lacked the appreciation of the great accomplishments of this great soul. I too, did not recognize the true extend of my father's greatness until his passing into the astral world, and I have matured as an adult. Everything that my father has foretold me has come to pass as predicted and to this day, I feel his presence and hermetic guidance.

My father's solicitude has been misinterpreted and pure egotism and pride of some students sadden my father at times.

However, my father's main concern was the hermetic development of his students. As a matter of fact, he saw his students' development as his main mission in his life. To achieve his goal, my father demonstrated superb patience and endurance and his love and dedication for others and went so far as overstepping karmic boundaries for his "Hermetic League Circle".

Moreover, I am filled with gratitude that I may now continue Seila Orienta's mission to publish his writings that will bear fruit and prove indispensable in the future.

Seila Orienta's closest confidantes, to whom I may count myself, continue Seila Orienta's mission under his guidance so that every conscientious hermetic student may escape the quagmire of the material world to find the strength and resolution to successfully and confidently walk the golden middle path.

That is my father's legacy.

Book I

My Life

1.

My Present Incarnation

My extraordinary life on the earthly plane began on January 14th, 1951. Before I was able to form my own memories of my childhood, my parents told me that I had been alert and awake mainly during the night hours. During daylight hours I had slept the day away soundly and tranquil, but once the sun passed behind the horizon, I arose rested and full of energy. Thus, was my life's structure until I turned six years of age.

At that time, my father fell ill and convalesced more than a year in various hospitals and spas. One day, as he was released from the hospital, he raised his voice in anger at me. Without hesitation, I threatened him with a rock in my hand. My aim was correct and the projectile soundly struck his head, which compounded his anger as he sought to punish me. He and I wore shorts as it was summertime and I ran through a large patch of stinging nettles with my father close at my heels. Not one of the stingers caused harm to my legs, but my father ceased his pursuit in pain and stinging agony.

I enjoyed a Catholic upbringing and at age nine I met a devout and saintly pastor who solidified my faith in the Divine.

However, churches and mass caused discomfort in my very soul as I preferred to pray the Lord's Prayer "Our Father who art in heaven" in quietude surrounded by nature, for I did not want to pray in crowded churches. During the prayer, I imagined the Lord in heaven figuratively, that I felt a personal connection to God. Once I spoke the phrase "Give us this day our daily bread" I held out both hands for the Lord to place something in my hands. Only what I received was not bread and the Lord, then said in my mind, "one cannot live by bread alone," and I was content. With the words "forgive us our trespasses," I practiced introspection and promised to give up a favorite toy for penance.

This way I lived a life in harmony with my faith. The prayers enabled me to feel close to God and felt blessed with intuition and inspiration. This wonderful harmony lasted throughout my childhood.

During my adolescence I gave the impression of being just like anyone else. Early on, I discovered an undeniable ability to influence my average peers, demonstrated a solid faith and a well-balanced character. On the day I saw my future wife for the first time, I said to her brother that she would become my wife, even though I didn't know her. In the long run, all plans I hatched came to fruition.

Somber days had cast a dark and heavy shadow upon my spirit. Sometimes the heavy hand of fate made it difficult to live on day by day. Fate had cast my entire family down into a morass of misfortune, leaving us with just the naked necessities of life. Years of misfortune and malaise forced me into the depth of despair, a condition that I would wish upon no one.

Many trials in my life stayed to this day and only my strong belief in my Godhead and my path towards the light enabled me to walk confidently through all encumbrances of my existence. Karma unleashed a never-ending storm as I navigated through my life, but in the long run, I learned to master what fate has thrown at me and mastered to stand firmly on my feet, despite the storm. After all, I had caught a glimpse the light that shone as a distant beacon in a far distance as I held on to my life raft of faith in God and in the confidence of soaring into comforting heights within the light world that lie ahead. With Franz Bardon's wise guidance, I found the tool to realize and fulfill my calling in this life.

Initially, I abused my gifts for nefarious purposes in my younger days. For example: As a young man, I was drafted into the army, and spend some days in the stockade for various infractions. One evening, when I smoldered in my cell once again, I hypnotized the security personnel and ordered each guard to hand over his weapon and I had the key keeper unlock the cell before I had all succumb to a deep slumber. Naturally, I repeated this prank every night since none of the personnel had any recall of the incident the night before. This was, in fact, just the beginning!

After serving my term in the army, I lived in Dortmund-Marten for some time, where I studied "Practice of Magical Evocation" and decided to evoke a being from the Venus sphere. Since I have not worked with being of the lower spheres in the first place, this evocation proved to be a difficult undertaking. For this reason, I decided to work with a medium. Soon I found a suitable person who would serve as a medium. In a basement room, I hypnotized my medium and after entering into a state of trance, I ordered my medium to locate a being called Hagiel.

Endowed with a great imagination, I immersed myself into a universe of indescribable vibrant green color, which cannot be found on our earthly plane. Within this sea of green color I petitioned my Godhead to stand by me. Once I felt at ease with my surroundings, I called out Hagiel's name into this sea of green light. I imagined her sigil in my mind until I sensed the approach of a great queen. Suddenly, I realized that my mental body was incapable of withstanding the oscillations of such a great being. The imagined sea of light began to fade. Hastily I loudly chanted Hagiel's name again and again. Once my consciousness reached the material world again, the medium opened his eyes and spoke with an altered feminine voice: "What do you want from me? Your actions pose an infraction of the universal law!"

I retorted that my evocative abilities are limited to using this process and that she may forgive me for my actions. Hagiel scolded me over the fact I used a male medium rather that a female one, which would be only appropriate when calling a female spirit.

"Are you really Hagiel?" I queried.

"If you need proof on my authenticity," she answered, "what do you desire?"

At this moment, someone knocked at the basement window that faced the curb outside. I opened the window and invited this nosey young man to join me at my undertaking. Once the young man faced the medium, which executed some gesture with his hand, the young man fell into a deep coma for 30 minutes. When he awoke, he fled the basement room in panic and fright. From this time forth, I was able to operate without any such disruptions.

Over time, I found 12 people to practice evocations around my medium. I spent the next two years harmoniously, filled with wonderfully strange experiences and one true evocation of a spirit being. At this time I gradually gained psychic power, just as my faith began to wither.

Our group of seven adults and five juveniles founded a circle I called "Bardonkreis" (Bardon-Circle League). The older members felt that honor and authority ought to be bestowed on them, rather than myself as the founder of the circle that caused much friction and discord among the members.

Hagiel withdrew and a demonic being filled her vacancy. Hagiel did not neglect to inform me of her departure from our circle's influential sphere. At this time on, I rarely joined any meetings. I began to undermine the circle by being in steady contact with this demonic being. Soon after, my contact with the demonic being began bear unexpected fruits.

I participated in a circle meeting and demanded to act as a medium. Immediately, chaos wreaked havoc among the members. One member, a 22-year old woman, ran hysterically through the room and lifted a 600-pound wooden cabinet off the floor at one end. The cabinet almost collapsed due to its own weight. Another member left the room panic-stricken by bursting through the closed door, thus destroying it. Yet, another member lifted the sofa together with four cowering occupants into the air.

I ended these horrific activities and informed the remaining members of the kind of being the group has associated with. In the end, this event broke our circle permanently. The medium was still possessed by the demonic being, which I exorcised only through great effort and the help of a more elevated positive being under the condition that the details of the exorcism shall not be revealed.

2.
A New beginning

After I lost contact with Hagiel and some other beings of the earth zone, I began to feel an inner emptiness and discontentment. Due to karma, my mental and astral awareness began to fade. To improve my condition, I searched for recipes for the creation of magick salves and fluid condensers aiding the detachment of my mental matrix. This way I invented an excellent elixir that enabled my mental body to exit my physical body at a moment's notice. Needless to say, the use such elixirs proved to be highly toxic as well as detrimental to a decay of my health. All this experimenting resulted in an extended hospital stay and an elemental shift within my mental body caused arbitrary separation of the matrix. Although I learned much about the astral plane at this time of my life, I found myself at risk of permanent damaging my health. On the other hand, I communicated with lower astral entities as well as with diseased individuals and travelled the panes at my own leisure.

As my body slowly began dying, I found myself mentally thrust into the heights of the mental sphere where I made the acquaintance of three beings, which ultimately saved my physical life. At my arrival, these beings led me into a triangular room, whose left wall was covered with unfamiliar symbols. One of the beings informed me that this wall represents my past. The wall in front of us was covered in symbols as well. Again, I was unable to decipher the symbols of the central wall. I noted that these symbols oscillated a disquieting ambiance upon my psyche. The second being, which appeared to be a magos of high ranking, pointed to the central wall and said: "As you can see, this center wall is only partially covered with symbols. This wall represents your present life. Your present lifestyle will sabotage any future progress of walking your path. Therefore, nothing more can be written on your wall of present life. Needless to say, the right wall, which represents your future, will remain blank, as you would have wasted your opportunity. This center wall, your present life, proves to be of paramount importance since it may profit your future. The right wall symbolizes your future. You may not be aware of this, but the future will also have some bearing on your present life. So I urge you to weigh the karmic consequences of squandering your life in such a manner."

Understandably, I was shaken by these harsh, but honest words. As I glanced quietly at my unfinished life, symbolized by the right wall, the third being broke the momentary silence: " You have accepted an important mission that best suits your character. Awake from your stupor so that you can see your true self! You have burdened yourself with negative karma. Learn from your past misdeeds and your mastery thereof, and teach others who want to study the hermetic sciences. Lead your students by example and illustrate how fate will mercilessly penalize any missteps in life."

As soon as the last words faded, I found myself alone in this triangular room. Sadness filled my heart and an image of Master Arion slowly materialized before my eyes as he instructed me to set up a circle for true hermetic students. He conferred abilities to me and called latent abilities to my attention. From this moment onward, my mission became apparent and I took an oath to fulfill my destiny. Once the images faded from my sight, I saw that the center wall was completely inscribed by symbols that gradually flowed onto the right-sided wall. I genuinely wanted to fulfill my mission in this lifetime.

Once I returned to my physical body late at night, I noticed my wife was awake and sitting upright, staring at an apparition that unfolded before her eyes. Master Arion stood at the foot of the bed. He was dressed in the fashion of an Indian holy man, wearing a white turban on his head, silently fixing his eyes upon us.

This experience rang in a new phase of development. I diligently practiced the first two steps in "Initiation into Hermetics," and gradually worked through exercises step-by-step. Although some exercises proved to be extremely difficult to master. Through intense introspection and all the willpower I was in the position to muster, I successfully balanced my character and all elemental disturbances that were caused by my previous lifestyle.

In due time, I gathered some of Bardon's former students, sometimes under extraordinary circumstances, while traveling to various countries. The first of Bardon's students with whom I established contact, was Rah Omir Quintscher's son Ernst Quintscher. I also encouraged my wife to seek correspondence with Maria Pravica and after some correspondence, I visited Irena Novakova in Prague, because she had much of Bardon's unpublished material in her possession. I also visited a gentleman in Prague who gave me the illustration of the 4th Tarot Card. All these former students had fond memories of Franz Bardon, his selfless service to mankind and his great deeds from which his students profited greatly. During my travels, I befriended Dr. Lumír Bardon, Franz Bardon's only son and also Bardon's purportedly favorite student, Dr. Milan Kuman. This way I gathered much knowledge of the work that Franz Bardon bequeathed upon mankind. Since many manuscripts I found were written in Czech, I had them translated into German. All these activities solidified my resolve to fulfill my mission to create a new study circle that I called the "Bardonkreis des Bundes (Bardon-Circle League).

Now, it was time to place advertisements for our Bardon-Circle in various occult and spiritual periodicals. As a result, I received hundreds of queries and ultimately chose twelve practicing students, who lived almost exclusively within a narrow radius of the circle's base in North-Rhine-Westphalia. These members now constitute the "Inner Bardon-Circle".

Throughout this time, my wife turned out to be of invaluable assistance in every phase of the creation of the circle.

3.
My First Mago-Mystical God Experience

Once I successfully completed all steps of Bardon's *Initiation into Hermetics*, I made my acquaintance with my guardian spirit. Much to my surprise, I noticed that my guardian spirit was none less than my former Tibetan guru from an incarnation two lifetimes ago. During that incarnation I often taunted my guru, ridiculed him before my fellow students and by committing misdeeds and exacerbated his daily life. Now that I was able to see his radiant aura, I recognized his advanced hermetical rank in the hierarchy. This new insight caused me to be filled with remorse for all misdeeds I committed in times past. However, my new former mentor embraced me forgivingly as he uttered the words: "You have always been my favorite protégée."

My guardian spirit supported me in the creation of the Bardon-Circle League. Furthermore, he revealed that Master Arion had chosen 28 students, whom he personally instructed, to guide and tutor others in hermetic principles. Those 28 adepts live all around the globe. I was called upon to instruct 14 students step-by-step to the portals of initiation. During a lengthy meeting, my guru urged me to choose a personal Godhead. He disclosed exact instructions in meditation techniques to realize that goal. While in meditation, which lasted six hours, a wonderfully bright golden light veiled my consciousness and I experienced a tetra-polar ecstasy, a conscious exposure to the four principal divine virtues. I am truly at a loss for words to describe this wonderful experience, which may have lasted mere moments, or many hours, since all references of time faded from my consciousness. During this ecstasy, I experienced my personal Godhead and the God from my childhood as one entity. The presence of this wonderful cosmic Godhead, which took and on an abstract form, filled my heart with humility; all surrounding sceneries were of an abstract nature that words couldn't describe. Although, in my mind I understood that there exists no higher God aside this magnificent God, I instinctively knew that Metatron may expand beyond that which is beyond. Such concepts are truly incomprehensible to the human mind. Alas, I am not authorized to say any more about this.

This exceptional divine encounter brought about a perfect equilibrium of virtues within my very being and from this time forth, I never felt alone. My Godhead was always present and I had no need for prayer or petition before God. Humility and reverence eliminated all my wishes and desires due to a constant stream of the reception of divine virtues. My Godhead and its omniscience diminished all earthly needs and desires.

Now I had the freedom to travel the astral plane at my own leisure. These travels gave me the opportunity to gather profound wisdom and mago-mystical secrets. I also began to personally see the students of the circle, an activity I indulge in to this day. This way, I was able to take care of imbalances within their character, and soon I began to consider them my children. I am still at their disposal and cater to their individual needs. However, I detest being the subject of veneration or devotion, a privilege reserved for Divine Providence. God's love shall fulfill all his children's wishes and give to his children what they need. Since I partake in God's love, I too shall give where I can. The more an individual opens his or her soul to me, the more I am willing and able to do for them. I will always give my all to help inexhaustibly. My love stands above karma and I do what I can to minimize my children's karmic burden. Although, I have to suffer the karmic consequences of eliminating or easing the weight burdening my children in their lives, nothing shall stop me from guiding my friends toward their goals. Once I have permanently exited this world, I will continue to guide the members of the circle unobtrusively.

4.

Parmasa

I clearly remember when I mentally visited a principal called Parmasa from the zone girdling the earth. My choice for selecting Parmasa was the fact that he is sympathetic to humankind. After preparing myself mentally, I called out his name several times, but to no avail. So I kept calling his name repeatedly, until suddenly I felt a tap on my shoulder, and a voice said, "you can call my name a hundred times, but you won't see me if you don't turn around!"

Parmasa is quite cheerful and humorous and he prefers to appear from behind. As I turned around, I gazed into a friendly face that changed its appearance every few moments. Some features were quite bizarre like expressions from cartoons that left me laughing out loudly.

"What can I do for you?" he asked me briefly.

I first asked him to be less cheerful, so that my laughter won't distract me from my request.

"Your wish is my command," he uttered as his face disappeared and only a gigantic nose appeared on his neck without a head.

I pulled myself together and spoke, " A member of our circle is contemplating suicide, and I seek your help." While I continued explaining my wishes, Parmasa's nostrils seemed to grow larger and alternated its girth. Although I sought out this being to help with a pressing matter, I began losing confidence in this being's ability to help.

"Well," he said, as he pulled a crown from underneath his cloak and placed in upon his gigantic nose, "I will help your friend." As he faded away, he muttered his final words: "Have we become the laughing stock of humankind, now?"

I thanked him, and once I returned to the physical world, I received some encouraging news about my friend. Astonishingly, within a short time, he became more cheerful and even met a lovely girl. Altogether, his luck seemed to have changed for the better.

5.

Chanting Mantrams

The material about mantrams that I received in Prague proved to be useful on many levels. There are forty-nine mantrams, of which eight were chanted without sigils. All mantrams consisted of multiple sentences formed into one or more paragraphs and required a sacrificial offering to various Gods. The first one that I chanted required cake without the use of animal fats in its ingredients. The wording was quite poetic and in unison with universality. More than six hours were required to repeat this mantram in its entirety a thousand times. Within a few days I mastered certain fluidity in chanting this mantram and managed reduce the time to four hours for each session of a thousand repetitions, but all my efforts seemed in vain at first and due to a lack of any success, I deliberated abandoning this project. I decided to abandon my experiment after the sixth consecutive day of chanting. On the sixth day, after about 300 repetitions of the mantram, I felt a slight electrical current passing through my body, moving down to the my Svadisthana region.

As this sensation intensified during continuing chanting, I found myself struggling to maintain consciousness and chanting became a slur. I spend altogether eight hours in this state. Intuitively I understood that I am dealing with Shakti on a basic level since this particular mantram is dedicated to Shakti, who is the great Goddess Maha-Devi. Finally, I was certain: The Goddess has taken notice of me!

The next day I decided to continue with the chanting of the mantram, and to my surprise, after only repeating the holy text twice, I felt a warming tingling sensation that travelled towards my solar plexus. Coming from a distance, I perceived a muffled voice, without being able to understand any spoken words. After chanting for days, the words of the mantram automatically passed through my lips. The memorization of the words enabled me to direct my concentration on the voice, the words spoken by Maha-Devi. Finally I understood the words and I was granted to partake in many great experiences, when a sensation of perfect harmony expanded throughout my very being, without ever fading completely in the times to come.

On the 12th and final day of chanting I was privileged to experience something that was reserved for very few practitioners. The silvery light of a bright moon filled my room in and polychrome dots of light danced before my window. At first, I thought that my exhausted mind deceived me until I saw the outlines of a female being taking on solid forms. It was a Goddess in person. Her head was adorned by a semicircle of stars and her heavenly beautiful dress sparkled brightly through the moonlit room. I sat silently before this magnificent mother of all things and smiled graciously as she weightlessly stood before me. A whole spectrum of colors emanated from this apparition of Maha-Devi. Some of the sparks touched me and each spark evoked a different sensation in my soul. In quietude, I lived through this paradise-like experience of being in the presence of a great Goddess, who carried some Indian features in her appearance due to the nature of the mantram. Being aware of the grace and greatness of Maha-Devi that I would never be able to achieve throughout my existence, I thanked the universe for the privilege of being touched by the grace of such a magnificent being.

At last, the Goddess began to speak and with a lovely voice she explained to me the entire act of creation. Every word, although powerful enough to stir my entire being, oscillated divine purity and universal omniscience that seemed removed far beyond the capacity of my intellect. Through this experience, I realized the limitations and diminution of the human spirit. Maha-Devi's motherly love, an eternal unconditional divine love that resides beyond human sentience, filled every cell of my being. I literally bathed in the rays of her grace and purity when she gradually faded away into her majestic realm, not without leaving my spirit full of heavenly delight. Her image was firmly engraved in my minds eyes and I will recall her grace for all days to come and I often repeat to myself the words "I have seen her."

Although, I chanted a few more of the forty-nine mantrams and enjoyed great success, I concluded that this form of magic, which demands large amounts of time, a luxury not many possess in our modern times.

6.

The Keeper of the Threshold

On many occasions, I have been asked the question how a person, who is privileged with spiritual insights, adjusts to daily mundane life? Mundane life diverts much of the energy that one needs for spiritual endeavors. Everyday life is ruled by ignorance, irregularities and struggles that conflict with the harmony a hermetic practitioner requires for his or her practices. A magus, with spiritual experiences is confronted with the profound quagmire of day-to-day squalor in a coarse and abrasive material world. Whenever I travel the throughout the heights of advanced ethereal spheres, and in the end, find myself being thrust back into the oppressive darkness of the physical realm, I must develop an almost superhuman level of adaptability to overcome the daily evil that the negative principle doles out especially to hermetics and students of hermetics. It is the negative principle's task and ultimate goal to force the true seeker off the path or complicate an established hermetic's life. The task of the negative principle consists of an important aspect of evolution. Without this resistance and the strength a hermetic musters to overcome obstacles, builds a true character and willpower necessary to grow and move on to a higher existence. Thus, it is possible to develop properly in the physical world. Furthermore, it is pertinent that the hermetic, withstands all resistance from the destructive principle and persists in moving ahead on the path or accomplishes a mission given to the hermetic by Divine Providence. A human being such as the hermetic student consciously strives to ennoble body, soul and spirit to be prepared for a mission. The novice's primary mission is that of his or her own spiritual growth. By overcoming the many obstacles of daily life, I successfully executed all exercises required to advance magically.

One day while practicing intense vacancy of thought, I entered into the depth of infinity and became oblivious of the body, mind and soul. What remained was pure consciousness without thought or sensation. In this depth of nothingness, space and time ceased. I neither expanded nor contracted and remained in complete stillness, which is considered one preliminary step before omnipresence.

As I remained in a rapt of vacancy, I was stirred by a sudden presence that billowed termination and perdition. A being with eyes of yellow lurked in this eternal darkness and held my consciousness captive. Instinctively, I strove to avert my spiritual death through the hands of this being.

"What frightens you?" an abhorrent voice thundered through the darkness. "Do you wish do delve deeper and further, my son?"

Something I have never seen before, a truly horrid being

revealed itself before my eyes. I could not describe this being in mere words. Although, some hermetic books give some descriptions, nothing could have prepared me for such a sight.

The presence of this being taxed my consciousness to the point of loosing myself. I wrestled myself to stay alert and asked, "You seem familiar. What do you want from me?"

"I am saving you from yourself", the voice thundered. "You have approached me and I am telling you now: I will never leave you. At times, when you think that I am far away, I am near. I force you to grow or die; the choice is yours. Once you are able to look into my eyes without fear, you may pass by me across the threshold. Think about it!"

I was not going to argue with this being and the image once again faded into the darkness. Swiftly I gained my normal consciousness at the spot I was sitting on a chair with thick drops of sweat pouring down my face. I felt physically weak and sick. To this day I believe that this encounter almost terminated my life in this world.

The "Guardian of the Threshold" spoke the truth and despite my inner equipoise, I regained my strength only slowly. Although, despite the physical maladies that resulted in the encounter with this being, her warnings saved my live. To this day I suffer from severe insomnia and I am often forced to ingest sleep medication.

I mentioned this encounter as a warning to everyone who thinks that he or she may skip some exercises or even some steps in the process of hermetic self-initiation. The Guardian of the Threshold will make sure that no one who has not reached the proper level of maturity shall pass into higher planes. Although, most hermetic practitioners will end in failure or self-delusion (Lebenslüge), some will encounter this horrific being personally. I have no advice for those individuals, for they must act according to their best knowledge, should they face this guardian. I wish I could spare others an encounter of this being.

*I used the Latin term "magus" rather than the anglicized magus to differentiate between a magus of the hermetic sciences and entertainment trick-magic (P.W.)

7.

The Bardon-Circle League

At this point, I would like to divulge more details about the Bardon-Circle League (Bardonkreis des Bundes). As I mentioned before, there existed an informal Bardon-Circle League that was doomed to disbandment owing to the chaotic conditions under which it operated.

Years later, I was allocated to create a new Bardon-Circle League that is true to the teachings of Franz Bardon and universal law. I was also given a copy of a letter that Franz Bardon wrote to a friend in the 1950's:

"I would welcome the idea if the lot of my students and devotees would create formal circles of allegiance that represents the interests of true initiation. However, its members should refrain from discussions of personal affairs and matters of the private lives of its members. Such circle should be based on dealing with the hermetic progress of its members and any distractions could weaken the allegiance and may lead to the dissolution of a circle. In a positive atmosphere, things will progress accordingly and guarantee success."

I knew what had to be done. Essentially, our Bardon-Circle League is a secret society, which, opens to the public from time to time. Three years of diligent practice of the exercises in Bardon's Initiation into Hermetics are a prerequisite for membership admission into the Bardon-Circle League. Aside from discreteness, there are no prescribed rules and regulations. The names of the members are secret to the outside for their safety. Any attacks on our members are futile and I will personally retaliate any animosity towards the members of our league. I formulated the "Instrument of Accession" to our league with the following words:

The Bardon-Circle League

Founded on May 10, 1986
in Eschweiler, Germany

Any individual, regardless of status or esteem, who seeks the truth through theory and practice in accordance to Franz Bardon's teachings, shall be welcomed as a full member of our league. Although, league members are adherents to the hermetic teachings of Franz Bardon, no member shall be coerced to participate in the league's activities and members are free to forgo membership to our league at any time for any reason, in accordance to our creed of complete freedom of the individual. Man and women are of equal standing. The Bardon-Circle has no established schedule for meetings and members shall agree upon a time for a circle meeting. The circle operates in an autodidactic manner, where each member constitutes his or her own teacher. Should any individual member face insurmountable obstructions on the path, the Bardon-Circle League will provide an appropriate mentor to resolve certain issues. The Bardon-Circle League has no headmaster and each member has his or her rights but no obligations. Practicing students with outstanding abilities and maturity comprise the inner circle. God shall provide complete initiation into primeval religion and full support in their magical endeavors shall be granted.

Name: _____

Signature _____

The principal intelligence of circles, groups, associations and leagues has been mandated to arrange that all practicing members of the circle live in close proximity of each other. I may use my abilities to help. It is a great joy, helping someone to shed some of the burden that life places upon a hermetic student and granting wishes. At times, however, it is necessary to admonish a student in a least obtrusive manner to lead him or her back onto the path. Since I am a more giving nature, I am delighted to present my students with gifts of hermetic nature. If it were up to me, all of my students should be able to accomplish the first Tarot Card in this lifetime. Some students are introverts and do not open themselves easily. So I have to gently ease myself into their hearts by working unobtrusively in order not to unsettle their fragile nature. Instinctively, they perceive my sincere sympathy toward them. All that is in my mission. I have a lot of children, although they don't know that.

8.

The 28 Pupils of Master Arion

Master Arion chose his students from within the astral zone. Those chosen students were the ones that most emphatically lamented about the lack of opportunity to advance on a true hermetic path in our physical world.

True initiation is not an effortless path to master. We all know the laws: Something of great value has its price. I was tasked to find 14 pupils. The search was arduous and I applied my mental faculties to find some of those individuals, and used the same powers to keep the circle together.

It is my goal to lead all of my 14 students to an advanced level and guide the most gifted ones to Step VIII in Initiation into Hermetics. As long as I will live, I will guide my children, stand at their side in times of trouble, help the ones that stumbled and fell, carry them and comfort any one of my children, unlike the remaining 14 students of my counterpart in Greece, who have a heavier cross to bear. Their teacher does not guide and comfort them. They are left to their own devices.

Once my students pass away into the astral realm, the most gifted ones will be instructed further in the astral world and some will reach greater spiritual heights. Master Arion will admit those adepts into his palace and teach personally. Those adepts will reincarnate soon after their training is completed and carry out a mission on our planet, while others will remain in the astral world for a greater duration and receive further training. In the end, those adepts will also be received at Master Arion's palace. All 28 students will become excellent teachers and each one of those adepts will, in time, instruct 14 students of their own.

In this way, the hermetic seed is carried to fruition and many a magi will carry out a mission to prevent an earthly catastrophe. Earth will enjoy spiritual rejuvenation and shall be cleansed of the remaining refuse. Naturally, the task to reach this goal will be arduous and many adepts will experience humiliation at the hands of the ignorant, but will prevail in the end. Never once shall we doubt victory. We shall stand before God in humility, as he will guide us on our mission; his will be done.

9.

My Friend Kuluch

Eventually, while mentally travelling through the astral plane, an adept's may develop a curiosity for visiting the lower spheres where the mediocre individuals dwell. I once travelled through very coarse reaches of the incorporeal realm, where I noticed an orange-red landscape in the far distant. Although its albedo was low, this place sparked my curiosity. At once, I transposed my consciousness, and I arrived in a barren land of red mountain ranges, devoid of any plant or animal life. Naturally, I surmised that this must be part of an astral inferno. Later I found out that this entire world was the realm of one lonely being. While pondering about the purpose of this peculiar world, a large shadow jolted my attention and I gazed at a huge eagle soaring through the red sky. Immediately, I sensed that there is more to this eagle circling the blood red sky. In the astral sphere, all animal forms are friendly, peaceful and gentle creatures, so I called upon the bird to approach. Promptly the eagle swooped down and upon landing, it assumed human form.

Before me stood a being that radiated dignity and might, as well as deep sorrow and despair. I asked the being's name.

"I am the great Kuluch," the being introduced itself after a long pause of silence.

"How is it then," I asked while inspecting our surroundings, "that this world is so peculiar and desolate?"

Kuluch looked in my eyes and said: "How right you are, human. This is my personal realm. I am its sole inhabitant.

"Where are your servants and subjects, and how did you get into this situation?"

"I am a prince without subjects," he interjected. "There is no being inferior or superior. Loneliness is just my punishment for insubordination. In vain I search for God, but nowhere can I find my God for comfort and support. That is my karma"

"You must know," he continued with a bitter face. I was banished to a realm that is not my true home for I am a principal of the Mars realm. The form of an eagle symbolizes my past virtues. No creature ever visited in many hundreds of your earthly years. You are my first guest."

Magically, Kuluch was a very talented principle. Through him, I developed the ability to view past and future incarnations — although I never gazed into the future. As a distinguished advisor, Kuluch wisely guided me on the right path. This spirit possessed great many powers. His power enabled him to shield me from attacks by spirits or fellow humans. I often imagined that Kuluch's wrath could spell devastation to anyone that attempted to defy him. One of his many talents was the ability to guard against fire through his skilled use of the electric fluid.

For some time, I regularly visited Kuluch in his realm. He was always compliant to receive me, and in one conversation, he made it clear that he would receive some of my friends as welcomed guests to his world, as long as I would not bring females. Once, however, he made an exception to his rule. As part of our friendship, Kuluch stood by my friends in times of need. Under the pledge of secrecy, he gave me his personal seal to contact him at any time and location, even without leaving my physical body. Upon the completion of a ritual, contact was established immediately. I heard his spoken words coming from my solar plexus.

He instructed me of the dangers of the Mars sphere by creating an artificial Martian force field to simulate the altogether unpleasant oscillation of that sphere. A visit to the Martian sphere evokes strong feelings of aggression in the visitor's mind as well as a strong impulse for the lust for power.

Kuluch will not be marooned in his world eternally. Eventually, he will be permitted to return to the Mars sphere with full rank and honor and upon full rehabilitation, Kuluch will resume his missions once again.

After my contacts with Kuluch, I missed his naturally aggressive character that is prominent among the genii of the

Mars sphere. However, the close proximity of his temporary to our zone girdling the earth has somewhat calmed his natural personality.

I will always appreciate Kuluch's friendship and close bond that has developed over time.

10.

My Visit to the Moon Sphere

After completing my extensive travels through the zone girdling the earth, I naturally became aware of the other planetary spheres. Alas, I was not in the position to visualize these spheres clearly. After all, the earth zone is infinite and contains a myriad of degrees of density, beginning at the coarsest — almost material — level and, continuing eternally, it reaches higher and higher into unknown subtlety. The subtleness of the highest divine spheres cannot be described in human terms and even at the divine level contain infinite degrees of subtlety. Naturally, some levels, especially the lower ones are heavily populated whereas the finer levels are inhabited sparsely.

It is impossible to measure the earth zone in material terms of measurement such Astronomical Units (AU) or light years. It roughly could be measured in billions of light years. The structure of the earth sphere is dissimilar to the material worlds structure, therefore the concept is hard to understand in physical terms.

With the desire to explore further spheres, I sought out an earth realm genius named Urael, who explained the configuration of the lunar sphere. The moon sphere happens to be analog to our astral body, which explains the silver color of the astral matrix (silver cord). Within the moon sphere, one may recognize the negativity or passivity of the physical sphere. Thus are the physical influences of the moon.

While in the earth zone, I impregnated my mental body to the best of my ability with lunar oscillations, but could not match the exact color combinations necessary for a visit to the lunar sphere. Urael who holds the rank of a lord, assisted me in achieving the proper color oscillations.

Soon after, I was on the way to the moon sphere by rotating around my axis and finally ascending to the lunar realm. Lights that matched my mental body's oscillation began to flood around me while the image of the physical moon faded away. In his second volume, Franz Bardon describes the moon sphere as opalescent. However, when I entered the moon sphere, I perceived the entire color spectrum, whereas the magnetic or passive light colors demonstrated prominence.

Since the four elements and the Akasha principle within the lunar sphere possess a structure that does not relate well to the human mental body, a temporary disability of processing thoughts and mental movement in general prohibited any action. Urael, who accompanied me on my journey, elucidated that this temporary process illustrates, to what extent the soul is bound to the mental.

Finally, after what appeared to be an eternity, I regained

my thought faculties and the ability to move about. After such experience, I realized just how painful it must have been for the proto-humans to move into an astral body. Due to the astral body's characteristics, the immortal mental body has become a mere reflection within the consciousness of the astral vessel. Furthermore, I also felt that life and death cycles on earth are strongly influenced by the moon sphere. The lunar sphere stands in opposition to the solar sphere, which maintains and enlivens the mental matrix. Needless to say, I initially considered this sphere quite depressing.

"We are only on the coarsest level of this sphere," my spirit companion responded to my thoughts. "Just like within the earth sphere, there are more subtle levels of this sphere as well. Also, your consciousness is not yet functioning properly and that still taxes your judgment."

After conditioning myself, my mental eyes began to adjust to the lunar conditions and I was in the position to discern details within my surroundings. For example, I noticed male and female lunar beings. Their features are similar to those of earthlings. There are female lunar beings, such as Ilue, who are extraordinarily beautiful. No earthly woman could compare with her beauty and grace. "Oh magus", I thought to myself, "beware of such beauty. It could spell your doom."

Much to my relief, Urael took the precaution of cloaking our presence. Although, pictorial language or imagery is universally the same on all spheres, I would have been quite incapacitated to converse, due to my diminished mental capabilities because of this unaccustomed environment. This way, our stealthy presence liberated me from the predicament of striking a conversation.

While observing the lunar beings at their activities, I noticed, much to my astonishment, a wonderful being passed by and faded into the subtler regions. My guide explained to me that this being was a human magus who routinely visited the higher regions of the lunar sphere. That which appeared a routine for one being, seemed to be an impossible feat to perform at this time.

Soon, unfamiliar oscillations depleted my mental body and exhausted I descended back to the earth sphere. Everything here radiated familiarity. I truly felt at home in the earth zone and the elements quickly revived my mental body.

I thanked my guide. Without the assistance of Urael, I would have had to work for years to gain access to the lunar sphere. This first visit to the moon sphere showed me God's magnitude.

I later realized that I could not have moved to the higher lunar level owing to my mental body's constitution at that time, since I could not have withstood the finer oscillations. However, after repeated visits, my mind began to recover its former strength. In order to communicate with a higher lunar intelligence, one must visit the moon sphere on at least 10 separate occasions to condition the mental body to the oscillations of a higher being.

11.

Involuntary Magical Homicide

A gentleman, who was a member of our old circle, visited my home on a regular basis. He possessed a gift for magic and was considered a master of imagination. Alas, this man kept contact with the very demon that I utilized for destroying the old circle. Whenever we met, this man feigned friendship and expertly hid his secret attraction for my wife from me. Within a short time, a spirit being I had conjured brought this secret to my attention. At his next visit, I confronted him openly about his attraction and our supposed friendship ended in a bitter conflict. From this day on, this man attacked me with his supernatural powers and the help of his demon companion. However, I averted his attacks without retaliating, until I realized that he intended to annihilate me.

Now, it was about time I had to act. I thought it would suffice to create a volt that contains a command that would diminish his desire for my wife. This volt worked well for about two years until his desire to possess my wife flared up even stronger, despite the fact that he had a lovely wife. Somehow he realized that I influenced him hermetically through a volt. His knowledge of being unable to terminate my life and the fact that I am able to create powerful volts that would frustrate is supernatural endeavors evoked great hatred and anger in this man heart. He became most determined to reach his goal. His urge grew exponentially and he began stalking my wife while I was off at work.

My wife confronted him and promptly rejected his desire. Angrily he stomped off threatening my wife: "If I can't have you, no one shall have you." Undoubtedly, he revealed his plan to use his powers to murder my wife.

Coincidentally, I became ill at this time and in my weakened state of health, I was unable to protect my wife hermetically. However, I approached some friends in the astral sphere and pleaded for support. Alas, not one of the beings was inclined to help due to my present Karma that I accrued because of a pact I had sealed some centuries ago. My faculties were hampered by frustration: my wife could be dead soon, had I not found a solution, and promptly, the first symptoms of magically induced ailments took hold of my wife. Initially, I was able to divert some of the worst symptoms.

In my state of despair, a demon prince came to mind, with whom I had close contact a long time ago. Although my past encounters with the demon in the past, carried more selfish motives and the story did not end well for me then. I had no choice but to approach this prince and seek help. Once I arrived in his realm, his subordinates led me into his demonic palace and before the throne of the demon prince.

It became apparent that every being here knew about my requests, by looking into their faces.

Surrounded by a golden light, Samael the demon prince received me from atop his throne. For this occasion he appeared in human form and donned a violet robe that was interlaced with threads of pure gold. Upon his brow, he carried a mighty crown.

"Come hither, little human", Samael condescendingly addressed me. "In times past, you have served me well. Thus I will grant you a favor and terminate a human life for you."

"Oh Royal Highness", I answered. "As always, you are well informed. However, I do not wish death upon anyone."

Disappointed he glazed at me and said: "Well, what do you want then? I followed this whole ordeal you and your wife had to endure. Wouldn't death would be the only true option to stop that man permanently?"

"Honorable prince", I replied, "I am quite aware of the cosmic laws of cause and consequence. In the end, I would find myself in your clutches if I agree to your solution to my problems."

"So, what are you thinking about?" Samael asked, feigning ignorance. I was well aware that he knew exactly what I wanted. He stalled this audience to gain more time to place his demonic influence on me. Needless to say, I was eager to leave this oppressive environment.

"Should Mr. D.B. continue his attacks on my wife", I dictated swiftly, the same afflictions that he bestowed upon my wife should befall his wife."

"This contract should come into effect, once I cast it into flames", I added demandingly.

Samael agreed and I returned to my physical surroundings. I immediately prepared two contracts, both for myself, because I never intended to accept the demon's service, otherwise I would have been in Samael's debt that would carry karmic consequences. So I carefully planned my steps for the next day. Overnight, Samael placed his signature and seal on the prepared contracts. On the following day, I paid a visit to my former friend. I presented him the contract with seal and signature. He smiled nervously, but in his excited state, he did not recognize the signature of Samael in its abbreviated form.

Within a week's time, my former friend's wife suddenly died. Perturbed by the death and the fact that Samael had not followed our agreement, I visited him, with both agreement forms at hand, at his palatial residence in his realm.

You have not kept your word", I burst out agitated, " and violated our agreement which I hold in my hand. That woman is dead. You have killed that woman without my consent.

I am not responsible for what happened. You are the one who murdered without decree."

Samael laughed aloud and said: "Don't be such a wimp. The woman is dead and justice took its course. Why all this commotion?"

Your version of justice took its course", in interjected swiftly.

"Now I am being reproached for doing favors?", Samael said. He glowered at me and hissed sardonically: " Take heed of those contracts. They may burst into flames." He knew that he had no recourse against me.

Although I didn't create any negative karma for myself and escaped a pact with Samael, I felt deep compassion for the dead woman and effectuated hermetic methods to elevate the woman's existence in the astral sphere, because she would have remained on earth for another 20 years, which were taken from her. I had no astral contact with her since she remained in an unconscious state. Such is the law of the astral sphere. Similarly to suicide cases, she will awake, once the 20 years have passed.

After his wife's death, my former friend's health and mental condition gradually worsened. He spent his time in casinos and his children turned bad. His life has become unbearably miserable, but that was his cross to bear in this world. I could not have intervened.

Only later I discovered that Samael not only served me, but also simultaneously aided my former friend though one of his subordinates. Samael was the winner, any which way the case may have turned out. This case demonstrated the clear intellect and cunning strategy of this demon prince. No matter how this incident may have played out, Samael had his way.

12.

Lodges, Societies and Peculiar People

Due to their spiritual prowess, some individuals find comfort in the presence high-ranking demons. It is not just the negative principle that draws these individuals close, but also the bright divine emanation these demons cast upon black magi, like a moth is drawn by the light of a flame only to find certain death.

Over the years, quite a few of such black magic individuals knocked at my door. However, I refused no one.

The Saturni Lodge is in reality a Freemason Lodge that has long passed its zenith. For this reason, the Freemasonship views the members of the Saturni lodge unsuitable for their purposes.

Sorting through my extensive collection of lodge materials, I found that it was not complete. To complete my collection, I sought a meeting with a Freemason of the 33rd degree, to arrange an exchange of writings. I was willing to pass on some materials that were of interest to this gentleman.

We met on a rainy Saturday in a quiet pub in Bochum

(Germany). To my surprise, Mr. W. turned out to be a charming and agreeable person. Right away, he explained his leaning to the left path, although he did not wish to discuss details. We exchanged materials and in our conversation that followed the exchange, Mr. W. attempted to convince me of the advantage of becoming a member of his organization.

I, of course, negated his query, stating that I have found my spiritual path and I see no reason to leave my path. I was not certain, what this man saw in me, but he offered me the opportunity to pass over the lower ranks and become a member of the 18° degree (Gradus Pentalpha — Practices of "Sexual Magick"). However, I negated again, and Mr. W pressed on: "Imagine you were a tree and all other trees around you would protect you."

"A solitary tree grows stronger and healthier that its counterpart in a forest", I retorted. "A single standing tree defies storms and can develop freely, whereas a tree in the forest does not possess this opportunity."

"Would you like to master the first two Tarot cards in this lifetime?"

I gazed at him with astonishment when his facial features began to change. It seemed that he had a gleam in his eyes like I have never seen before.

"Would you like to join the Lodge of the Golden Century (FOGC)?" he finally queried.

"I am on the path of the middle", I responded acerbically, "and I am not willing to divert. I am honored by your confidence in my abilities and I respect you as a person. I will always remember you as a strong person who has found his way. "

After we parted, we remained in contact for some time, until the grand master under a threat of death terminated all correspondence. I responded by stating that I had no further interest in a contact with any members of the lodge and expressed mutual respect for each other's affairs; thus ended all contact to Mr. W., whose lodge name was Frater Giovanni.

13.

The Order of the Templars

One day, I received a telephone call from someone in Bonn (former capital of West Germany). A friendly voice asked, if I owned materials from a secret book written by Rah Omir Quintscher that I had received during a visit to Quintscher's son Ernst. I was quite confounded by this caller's knowledge of my visit, so I arranged a meeting with this mysterious person.

Days later, my doorbell rang and as I opened the front door, a well-dressed man, donning a pointed goatee, the external sign of a member of the Templar order whose members revere Baphomet as their supreme Godhead, greeted me politely. His outer physical appearance and gestures did not reflect his inner emanations, which I perceived as being quite unpleasant.

Nevertheless, I invited him inside. We spent a few minutes with the usual pleasantries and general talk about the Templars who originated from the Maltese Order. Without further ado, my visitor disclosed that he wanted the signatures I possessed of all the negative genii of the mercurial sphere as well their effects in relation to the elements and the electromagnetic fluid.

"I know about your Godhead", I responded slightly piqued. "He is powerful and he could reveal the information to you desire. So, why do you ask me?

"Well", he blurted out freely, "our Godhead does not want to reveal this information at this time."

"Don't you think that this circumstance has something to do with karma? I smiled as I leaned backwards. I could feel his hatred and aggression, which he so carefully hid behind a gentle smile.

Suddenly a jolt of anger took control over his composure. "We will terminate you with our Tepaphone," he hissed.

Taken aback, I considered throwing him out, but I decided to employ a different strategy. As a pretense I quietly assumed a pensive posture, while I gradually withdrew my guest's life force. Dark rings formed under his eyes as he hunched his back wearily.

"Do you know anything about life rhythm?" I said, breaking the silence.

He began to shake as I just slightly disrupted his life rhythm. I saw the fear of death in his apprehensive eyes. My Templar friend literally struggled for his life. Sweat poured down his face and his breath labored as that of a dying man while his heartbeat began to weaken.

"Let that be a warning to you and your brethren", I added firmly. "Where is your God now? Has he forsaken you?"

I revived him by adding Prana to his matrix to prevent a complete breakdown of his system, ultimately resulting in his death. His heart gradually became stronger and energy revived his very being. As soon as he gathered enough strength, my "friend" silently made a dash for the door.

14.

Dispersal of a New Age Group

In a new-age magazine, called "Esotera", I noticed an advertisement for an open group gathering of the "Association for Life Counseling and Reiki" in the town of Gelsenkirchen. I was curious and since the meeting took place nearby, I went and signed up for the meeting.

The head of the group was a somewhat plump woman, who also ran a business as a real estate developer, and her male associate, who worked as a district manager for some travel agencies. The third of the group was another woman who was a professor of electro-physics. All other members present appeared to be less flamboyant individuals. However, the aura of the entire group was awash with self –praise and self-aggrandizement.

No one in the group knew my name and when asked, I declined politely. The group discussed the opening Reiki centers for profit, even though it seemed that all the members here were well endowed financially.

As I listened to the discussions, I realized that Divine Providence had sent me here to uncover the pure avarice of a group that operated under the guise of helping others in need.

I feigned chronic pain that inflicted my wrist and the lady in charge asked one of the group's healers to tend to my affliction. Although I sensed the aura of this healer, I felt no life energy coming from this so-called him. Finally, after a few minutes of Reiki, the healer asked: "Does this help?"

"You should know", I replied, "you are supposed to be the Reiki master, aren't you?"

I was quite incensed by this group's pretentious attitude. "I am an advanced Reiki master", I blurted loudly. "Reiki is based on the electromagnetic fluid.

"Why don't you try using electricity?" the woman in charge responded.

"Not a problem", I said to her. I asked the lady to stand while I rolled up my shirtsleeves. Then, I held her hands, remarking that she should pay close attention.

A sudden jolt of energy pulsed through the lady's body, followed by a second equally strong jolt that threw her into her chair. Since my sleeves were rolled up, anyone was able to see that I did not manipulate the experiment through an external source of electricity.

The entire group surrounded their superior as she slowly

and quietly recuperated from the two electric jolts.

Once she had recuperated — only her disheveled coiffure showed her brush with an electric current —, the lady offered me a handsome amount of money if I were to join this group, an offer I politely declined. In the end, the entire group sheepishly admitted to the fact that they have never seen such a display of energy.

Once the lady restored her appearance, she queried about other abilities I could demonstrate.

"I read minds", I responded in a factual voice.

The lady grinned and with a slight tone of ridicule in her voice she said: "Well, read away!"

"My dear woman", I said, "for quite some time you are trying to coerce the manager from the travel agency to sleep with you, while your husband stayed home to tend your children. You called this meeting for the mere purpose of creating an alibi as a cover for a romantic evening!"

"Stop it!" she demanded while the entire group glanced at her in disbelief.

"Now, let's see", I continued without the intention to let her interrupt my reading. "I see that you, Mister manager, have noticed this lady's advances. You see yourself in bed with her, although you don't find her attractive. Your motives are purely financially. God help you, should your jealous wife learn of your intent."

The lady turned beet-red, while the man lost all color to his face.

Relentlessly, I continued: "Although you both know each other's ulterior motive, you will consummate your affair tonight."

"And you", I said as I turned to another woman, "you did not see this coming, even though your read cards? You must excuse me now. I cannot join such an incompetent group. I bid you a good night."

In a last attempt, the lady wanted my address, but I left without saying another word. My conscience was clear as I fulfilled my mission here. In the following weeks, I received news that the group was disbanded soon after that night.

Once upon a while, I encounter people, to whom I may demonstrate what hermetic magic can do. It is quite a delight to demonstrate the existence of magic to mature individuals since I usually keep my abilities secret. Silence is a power, which most individuals misunderstand.

15.

Bekaro, My Strict Teacher

I had traveled through several levels of the Zone Girdling the Earth, when I noticed a bright red star in the distant void of the astral skies. Once I trained my mind on the star. Immediately, I was greeted by a graceful genius: "I awakened your curiosity to visit this place because I have wished to see you."

I had to admit that this being had a sharp and powerful mind to alter my initial travel plans. Up to this point, I never diverged from my plans while traveling the astral sphere. At first I had no idea about the identity of this genius. Only later did I learn that my wife, Ariane, arranged this meeting.

This genius, which introduced himself as Bekaro, called me by my spiritual name and I became immediately aware of the importance of this meeting. Although Bekaro did not assume a human form, his appearance emanated charm and grace.

"You are a human who possesses a certain fervor", Bekaro said, "and that makes you the ideal leader for your group. Your passions are well balanced, actively as well as passively, and due to your personality traits, there will not be any repose for you until eternity."

Disheartened by these icy words, a dark veil of melancholy befell my soul. I asked myself: "Will I ever find repose?"

"Take delight in all your traits", Bekaro comforted me while he had read my thoughts, "Your abilities allow you to work efficiently in the world. Ariane, your soul mate, shall consciously represent the works of the great Master Arion.

Our next meeting will be in the physical plane. Prepare yourself well for this evocation. I won't reprimand any mistakes on your part. Should you have any difficulties, you may enlist the aid of your soul mate Ariane."

I was quite elated when all the preparations for the forthcoming evocation of Bekaro were done properly. Nevertheless, I checked and rechecked my list and ensured that everything was properly executed since this one was to be my first evocation of a high principal genius.

Once I stood in the magic circle, dressed in a silk robe and placed a crown on my head to demonstrate my rank as an adept. I concentrated on divine unity and proceeded by evoking Bekaro into the magic triangle before me. At first, few flickers of light danced above the triangle. Soon, thousands of specks appeared and formed into polychrome spectacles of astral light. Then, with a sudden explosive burst, the lights vanished and Bekaro stood before me in human form.

Bekaro's aura emitted an immense quantity of astral light that requires a magus to wear a robe of pure silk for protection. He stood tall in a royal robe of red and blue and a violet cape draped his shoulders. Upon his brow, he wore a crown of radiating gold that prominently displayed a large ruby and other gems, the likes of which I had never seen before on earth.

To my surprise, Bekaro bowed before me and made a gesture of veneration when he said: "I greet you and bow to you with all due respect. It is an honor to be speaking with you.

Without further ado, let me come to the point of this evocation. There lives a woman in Prague who harbors many writings of Master Arion. Your wife, Ariane, is aware of the existence of this literature. Go to Prague, seek out this woman and offer her a golden ring with three diamonds, which is in your possession. However, she will not accept the ring, but your gesture will soften her heart. Pay her well and she will give you whatever literature she has. I will leave you two of my servants to assist you, stand by your side and inspire you when necessary."

As I thanked Bekaro, two spirits appeared at his side. They were invisible to the untrained eye, but would not escape my clairvoyant vision. These assistants emanated oscillations of benevolence and power, similar to that of Bekaro.

Bekaro went to a greater detail about my mission to retrieve Master Arion's writings. During our conversation, he stressed that the virtue of justice must be applied in my undertakings, lest I wish to fail. At that time, Czechoslovakia was ruled by a totalitarian regime and many dangers lurked on the way to Prague. Bekaro's spirit servants proved to be invaluable and they guided me past the border control without having to endure the infamous baggage checks.

Once our meeting concluded, I thanked Bekaro and with a release gesture. Bekaro vanished in the reverse process of his appearance at the beginning of the evocation.

After this evocation, I meet with Bekaro many more times. He is kind and wise, but will be strict and relentless, should an individual commit injustice. In such cases, Bekaro demands immediate rectification. He proves to be quite adamant in his stance. Bekaro, endowed with sheer limitless power, can be quite convincing in forcing an adept to correct any wrongdoing, while his concern involves the maintenance of the equilibrium. Due to his rank and power, Bekaro's sphere of influence is vast and spreads widely across the astral worlds.

16.

A Lesson in Humility

There seems to be a law in human existence that the more an individual knows, the more questions will arise. I happen to be inflicted by this trait. Once the question arose as to how important and valuable my own life would be in respect to the rest of the population. Since I was not able to find a satisfying answer, I contacted my guardian spirit who shamed me for asking such a daft question. My dear guardian spirit had his ways to help me along to find my own answer.

Within a moment, my guardian spirit and I left earth until it appeared as a distant blue marble before my eyes.

"Now ponder upon this vision", said my guardian spirit.

I sat before this beautiful blue gem and pondered when I realized that I could not see any humans. They were too small to be visible, insignificant in relation to the grand scheme an entire universe. What role did I play? I would be insignificant and too small to see, just like our forefathers, all of earth's heroes, emperors. Nothing! I heard no laughter, no cries. I saw no artists creating masterpieces, composers writing beautiful music, literary minds creating immortal works or any other human achievements. All I saw was this blue gem.

"What do you see?" my guardian spirit said, interrupting my train of thoughts.

"I see nothing", I replied.

"Exactly! Where are those supposedly important things? Where are you and your ambitions? Can you see yourself on this earth before you? No human achievements, neither yours nor the accomplishments of your fellow humankind can be seen. Take a good look. This is how God sees you: invisibly tiny and insignificant."

His words shocked me deeply. Everything is nothing, utter significance? I realized that my thoughts were a manifestation of atheism.

"Indeed", he continued. "Your questions pose faithlessness to its core. You could have had positive results, had you not placed yourself at the center. Thus, your query was of a pure materialistic nature."

I had learned my lesson and I understood that any egocentric deeds and attitudes are without meaning. Egocentricity translated to a lack of faith, a desecration of the Holy Spirit by tainting all that is pure through the impurity of materialism. Therein lies a universal law and I reformulated my question: "How may I do justice towards God and how can I serve Divine Providence as a lowly creature?"

Upon reformulating my question, the picture before my eyes began to change. All planets seemed to interconnect harmoniously. I saw people existing in union with spirits. All the beings in the cosmos were striving towards Divine Providence. Then, I saw myself, small and insignificant, wearing a sign upon my brow. At last, I saw my true self.

My guardian spirit glanced at me affectionately and said: "Did you finally understand, what is important in an adept's life?" I finally understood spiritual maturity.

"I know that I make life difficult for you at times", he continued, "but that is my task to make you understand. In the future, I advise that you hold back your abilities to some extend; although use them when necessary. That is my wish."

I bowed before this loving, wise spirit and thanked him for his true guidance. I would follow his advice in acknowledgement my appreciation for my guardian spirit. At all times, I had to watch my thoughts carefully and keep my mind alert, thus avoiding earthly pitfall. All adepts, whether advanced or novice, must always be vigilant!

17.

A letter from a Student

Dear Anion:

Although I haven't written for some time, I haven't forgotten about you. I hope you and your family is doing well.

In recent times I thought much about my past visit in Castrop-Rauxel. It was and is important to me, and likely any other visitors that you do what you have to do.

I had long conversations with Kaya and Sven and I experienced much in recent times. Changes came about quickly. Last summer I took a job as a nurse for five months in Heidelberg and afterwards I travelled with my girlfriend to India.

In India I had a wonderful God encounter that gave me much energy, courage and motivation. You know, my dear Anion, that doing the exercises and battling one's vices is quite difficult. It is easier to win a thousand battles in war then it is to maser one's thoughts. I am sure that you don't want to hear about my daily battles, although I value your advice. Kaya, Sven and I speak about you often.

At the moment I am preparing for my naturopathic licensing test and will be taking my public health officer test in the summer of 1995.

Something big has been guiding my life for a while now. After my 5-month stint at a hospital, I became disillusioned by the lack of humanity found there and I couldn't satisfy my need to help others. I am shocked by the sheer avarice and dehumanization within the health field. All this negativity has caused stomach aches and intestinal disharmony. I quit smoking and I am avoiding any excesses.

My main concern at this time is introspection and thought vacancy. That is an adequate task and it keeps me occupied. I had trouble doing the exercises in Heidelberg and I lost control and physical ailments returned. Didn't you say that I would have a hard time? As hobby philosopher and seeker I often ask myself the question: WHY? Then, again I compare my life with others, jealousy gets the best of me and the feelings become hard to control. Maybe this question will be answered, as I grow older. Maybe it is good this way.

Often I wish Franz Bardon were here and would give me advice or guide me in the right direction. However, at times I even doubt that he truly existed. Oh, those old doubts! I think that I am having at least some control of my affairs at this time.

However, thoughts about evocation, charged mantrams and all advanced magic unsettle my mind. Logic dictates my mind otherwise. On the other hand, I noticed some latent abilities that most individuals harbor within.

Trying to avoid the illusion of being special turns into a daily balancing act. The study of hermetics is a hobby and often it is difficult for me to understand that I am overlooking the simplest things. You know that I found myself in a dark abyss.

How would I know if I don't do the exercises right? I absolutely despise the mechanical nature of the exercises and that it seems so forced upon, so authoritarian. How can I do the exercises, if I haven't fully grasped the theory part of the hermetics? I noticed, how much I have changed and I take delight in the changes that are to come. However, it is frustrating when my view of the world crumbles before my eyes. The certainty to walk towards the light is based on faith, I suppose.

I would really appreciate it, if you would have some time to answer my letter.

With Best Wishes, _____

The above letter should serve as a typical example of the many letters I received from people who seek my advice. Usually, my answers are strict and harsh to stimulate the mind of the seeker. Thus, the following words were my answer to the above letter:

Dear _____:

I take delight in hearing about your wonderful God encounter in India. I will not ask you about any details about it.

However, I fail to see why the path would seem difficult or that it seems easier to win a thousand battles than conquering one single thought after you had a God encounter?

However, I see it completely different: My very own God encounter enabled me to complete all my tasks effortlessly and face any disagreeable events confidently. Without a doubt, I find that it is easy to avoid negative thoughts altogether. God gave us the spirit (mental body) and it is our task to transform our human spirit into a Holy Spirit*. That is our all-important task on earth. We should not wait for opportunities to fall into our lap, but rather seek opportunities. You should be able to sense arising thoughts as they announce themselves beforehand and through the exercise of thought control, we should become familiar with our thought patterns, and to where our thoughts lead. Diligent thought control is the prerequisite to thought mastery.

Understand that you cannot battle thoughts because you will always turn out to be the loser. We simply allow negative thoughts to pass through us and away, or we send them away before they unfold in our minds, similar to a lightning rod that averts lightning damages by guiding a lightning strike down to the ground. Indeed, a proficiently trained student does not see thought mastery as a battle, but rather a "cakewalk".

That is quite different than an individual, who eagerly accepts and retains a destructive thought and materialize those thoughts through the matrices.

The problem is not to be found within the spirit, but rather within one's soul mirror. I have the feeling you are running from something in fear. Your problem is your character. As you can see, I like to keep my answers short and to the point.

One is hard pressed to find human decency in this world. It is best to become a decent human first; otherwise one cannot work hermetically later on the path.

By the way, inhumanity and avarice are pure ideals within their own rights since they enable us to counter humanely and generously.

You are an independent being and I urge you to clean house first, before you remove the rubbish before other people's houses. You mentioned that you are sick. Now you know the source of your ailments.

Preliminary hermetic training consists of introspection and thought vacancy, and if you hope to develop, you must work harder on yourself. A top athlete does not advance in competition without long and hard training. Without training, an athlete has already lost before the race begins.

Some time ago, I told you that you would experience a difficult period. Act accordingly and pay attention. The indirect path does not lead to success. Compare it to a book read through a mirror, which is an unnecessarily difficult task. Tread the direct path that leads to understanding; understanding leads to exercising and exercising leads to wisdom.

You are looking at your life through a mirror and read your life mirror-inverted. You wish that Bardon were here? That would not make a difference and ease and shorten your path. Again, you are deluded. Your development is something precious and not something that can be gained through trickery and shortcuts. You must rely on God. Whatever he gives is a gift, whether good or bad.

Please do not take Milan Kumar's words too seriously and call the hermetics a hobby. A hobby does not lead to completeness. Please find a better description.

It is not that you do not see the simplest things; rather the simplest things do not see you. Do things have ears and eyes or even intelligence? Use your own senses and intelligence.

The difference between a magus and an ordinary individual is that the latter lives consciously. Of course that is not a feat to be mastered within weeks or months. All things magical or mystical are of value. Material gold is precious. Imagine then, how precious spiritual gold might be?

You complain about the mechanical nature of the exercises. Think about it. Mechanics stand for order and control. There *would be no life without mechanics. You breathe mechanically and your heart beats mechanically, even though you do not think about it constantly. You place one foot before the other automatically. The entire universe is a mechanism. Life is a mechanism. So what is your problem with mechanics?*

Now a few words about your worldview: You are self-destructive and you will destroy your own philosophies as long as you ignore the universality of things. Just look at the stars in the night sky. See the harmony. Use this view of harmony and your God encounter and nothing can fall apart for you.

I hope you will master things, even if you dislike them. However, their truths are indisputable. Please read between the lines of this letter, then the harsh words will become loving advice. Read this letter with love because this letter was written with love.

God's blessings and success to you,

Anion

18.

A Necessary Spa Visit

After I was diagnosed with a disease caused by the bite of an infected tick, I had to visit a spa to convalesce. The disease affected part of my brain, especially my visual cortex and glandula pinealis, which resulted in impaired vision, migraine headaches and depression. The medical professionals prescribed potent pharmaceuticals to counter the effects. Despite all the pain and vision effects, I maintained a normal appearance to the outside world. Due to the disease's effects of pain and exhaustion, I had to quit work, although I used my willpower to train unaffected regions of my brain to substitute for lost regions.

Additionally, my wife was inflicted by a debilitating life-threatening illness. Since physicians were unable to improve her condition, I used my last reserves of energy to aid in restoring her health. It seemed that a social and financial decline became eminent. Despite these dire times, I never lost my trust in my Godhead, which led friends to help out financially, for which I am very grateful.

I found myself at the bottom and my physical life seemed to have lost meaning. However, I maintained my position as an advisor and mentor to some and offer stability and protection to others. I always helped wherever I found that I was needed.

When I arrived at the spa hospital, I was given a single room. I feigned ill-tempered characteristics. The staff would minimize any contact with me, in order to avoid an outburst of fury. This way, the staff would not barge into my room unannounced or cause unnecessary commotions.

All this was necessary to find proper tranquility to concentrate on a presage that hatched the feeling of some grand occurrence to unfold. My guardian spirit had demanded that I should leave all my amulets and talismans at home. He mentioned work with astral Akasha in order to receive a grand initiation onto matters that will exceed anything I had ever imagined.

One quiet evening I began to charge the large closet mirror in my room at the spa in Bad Salzuflen (a spa town in the German North-Western state of North-Rhine Westphalia). Afterwards, I retired to my bed to initiate the separation of my mental body. Once I freed my mental body, I swooped across the room to enter the mirror. When I passed through the surface of the mirror, I was surrounded by a familiar absolute blackness of the astral ether. Any uninitiated individual, who would visit this place, would find the Lady Guardian of the Threshold.

The astral ether is absent of time and space. It would not make a difference, whether a second, a day, or even a millennium would pass. Time has no authority. In this timeless and spaceless continuum of nothingness, I formulated my wish to know more about the Godhead of Christ. Once I formulated my wish, I found myself atop a hillside.

In the darkness of the night-like ether, I gazed upon the silhouette of a man as my ability to visualize was becoming stronger. I saw a man, who was a carpenter at one time, wearily sitting upon a rock. His face was filled with fear. I asked myself: Where was the Godhead? His twelve disciples slept in a near distance. At once I noticed why they did not keep watch at this weary hour. The air was laden heavily with trepidation, fear and depression. It seems that all the demonic beings united to besiege the poor and lonely carpenter with pain, scorn and ridicule. Since my presence is purely mental, I barely felt any of the emotions in the air.

I gazed into his gentle face, which was framed by a beard and long hair that draped over his shoulders and back. His deep eyes shone beautifully blue. When he noticed me and I fell on my knees in awe and love towards this great soul. I realized the sacrifice that this divine being made for humankind: He abandoned his union with God during his worst time, so that he was able to fulfill his mission as a mere human being, without the means and power to help his own self. Thus, as a man he was able to fulfill his mission to save humankind.

Deep compassion filled my spirit, when I gently stroked his feet to comfort him. Then, suddenly I felt a force thrusting my entire being upwards into a sea of colors, colors that I have never seen before. Gradually, these lights gave way to a steadily expanding bright golden light until it filled an infinite void without beginning or end.

A never-ending spectrum of rays of lights burst forth from this golden light. It seemed as if this light was connected to suns, planets and all planes and spheres of existence. Every aspect of the universe became united through this spectrum of unimaginable wavelengths of light. Universal laws began to fill my mind. A mighty voice broke through this spectacle and said: "I am the Christ, who cannot be found by human beings in their respective spheres. I took on the form for the ones who are mine, so that they may recognize and perceive me through their minds. Alas, since human perception is limited, they may only perceive a tiny portion of what I am, as I serve the grandest of the grand. Thus, I cannot be small. All twelve venerable Ancient Ones are homologous with my spirit. Henceforth, I exist on a different level of existence."

Soon after, I awoke in my physical body again. Once I stretched my limbs, I realized that dawn was near. This Christ experience, the realization of Christ's true force left a deep impression in my mind and soul. I encountered Christ while he experienced his worst moments on this earth, at a moment when he was only a man, a man as common as any in a moment of highest despair and fright.

My compassion for this Godhead prompted this giant among the spirits to initiate me in the cosmic laws that have never been written in this world. Blessed be this divine being. Ultimately, I realized that there were similarities between Christ's life and the life of the great Master Arion.

In the morning I took a cold shower to revive my spirit and when I dressed I noticed a faint hum in the room. "Now what?" I said quietly with an undertone of irritation. "Is one of my students doing something foolish again?" Clairvoyantly I inspected the aura of each student and came to the conclusion that all was in order.

However, I could not shake off this restlessness. I nervously looked around my room, when I noticed Master Arion. For some reason unbeknownst to me, he sat on a chair facing away. I looked at his shining black hair as I grabbed a stool and sat down. In the past 25 years, I encountered the Master only twice.

"That is good", Bardon said with a soothing voice, "you should not face me directly today."

Many thoughts entered my mind. I had to actively concentrate on bringing order to my mind, so I practiced thought vacancy to ban all thoughts from the periphery of my consciousness. As a result, I fell into a slight state of trance, but I once more became the master of my thoughts.

"You are fulfilling your mission admirably", the Master continued. "In spite of all misery you have encountered, you did not hesitate to support your students in their times of need. You are aware that individuals like yourself are not well-received by the negative beings. Nevertheless, you paid your respect, where it was due to the negative principle.

I know that you have grown tired of all of life's struggles. On many occasions I protected you and your students from extreme harm. Your wife, Ariane, knows me well and I have visited her many times. She is quite gifted and possesses many talents. I have conveyed advice and warnings through Ariane. Take heed of her advice and counsel. She walks the path of the universal laws and for this reason, she is part of the league. It is not her mission to lead as a master, but rather stand by your side.

Once your stay at the spa has ended, your mission will change slightly. Teach my students, who are under your guidance, more independence. You will initiate the most promising of my students in the Atlantean Rites. In this matter, I will rely on your intuition.

Both, my earthly son and my student, Milan, were once initiates. However, they were never given a mission and in time they had walked off the path. For that reason, you cannot rely on them for guidance. Fortunately, you possess all necessary skills to rely on yourself in the tasks ahead. Lastly, tell all the students who have a certain degree of maturity, where their place shall be, once they arrive in the astral sphere. This will help them to adhere to their given path.

So, my dear Anion, just like my brother Joshua, I shall leave you with a gift as well!"

Once the master had finished, I felt an upward thrust of my consciousness only to see the true greatness of Master Arion in his full glory. The cosmic void filled with blue gold. Colors and sounds guided golden suns, spheres and planes of existence to their proper places throughout an infinite cosmos. Everything that existed became interlaced with omnipresence, omnipotence, omniscience and omnisentience and established a rapport with Providence, an unpersonified Divine Providence. At this moment, a thought jolted through my mind, a thought that had no end: How can the unmanifested manifest itself?

When I awoke in my physical body in the middle of the night, I could feel my exhaustion throughout all three bodies. Only a Quabbalistic formula brought me back onto my feet quickly; although a pain in my back gnawed relentlessly throughout my torso.

This night I couldn't think of sleep. Excitement rushed through every cell of my being and my spirit was filled with light. Myriad thoughts dashed through my consciousness and brought bliss to my consciousness.

Thinking back to my recent experience, I concluded that these grand godly spirit beings are having not much in common with ordinary human beings. Compared to us humans, these giants belong to a completely different evolutionary level. They also underwent a developmental cycle quite different from us.

Although once they incarnate on our earth, they will adapt to all physical laws that rule the physical earth. This way, these high beings appear like ordinary humans.

However, from my perspective, they are cosmic forces beyond our comprehension, since they act exocosmic and heed only to Divine Providence and are a direct part of it.

Through his mission, Christ has, aside from other divine virtues, demonstrated omnipotence followed by omnisentience (all-love). As a god-like individual, each one of these giants is unique, and that fact is one of the 864,000 cosmic laws that were revealed to me. I did not have to memorize all these laws since that would be humanly impossible unless these laws were implanted in my consciousness by one of these spiritual giants.

Some of these laws pertain to spheres that are unknown to us and become apparent, once all Tarot cards have been mastered. After encountering all these laws, my mind is literally filled with thoughts about the laws' meaning and interpretations. For some time I had difficulties directing my mind to mundane affairs and I was developing a general disinterest toward earthly matters. However, through thought control and thought discipline, I redirected my thought stream to matters at hand.

All things considered, it is a great honor having been granted an insight to these cosmic matters, something I would consider quite unusual and extraordinary. In the light of these experiences I had to ponder the encounter of Chenresi — the one looking with clear eyes.

Chenresi, the embodiment of cosmic love, is depicted with one thousand arms that reach out to give aid and comfort to all suffering creatures. It is stated that Chenresi took an oath before the Emperor of Saturn not to rest until the last being has been saved.

Additionally, Chenresi, just like other Godheads, operates exo-cosmically. For this reason, the oath has also been made before Divine Providence.

The extraordinary dedication, sacrifice and engagement Chenresi demonstrates toward human evolution surpass human comprehension. However, in the end, Chenresi will be the oldest being located in the universe, one that has experienced many solar births and deaths. Kama

Although I have spent about ten hours in the realm of Chenresi, I have no words to describe my experience. Human words are limited our earthly existence. Ultimately, omnisentience — or all-love – is just another word in our vocabulary. In summary, the deeds of Chenresi are inconceivable.

In fact, all the great beings, such as Christ, Buddha and Maitreya, that walked upon this earth, predicted their return. Depending on legend, their return should occur in the course over the next 30,000 years. However, these beings will return within the span of the next 4000 years or less. At that time, the hermetics will have become a world religion and Akasha will have a stronger influence upon the individual human beings in the material world. In other words, humankind will be more balanced in character. By then, a benevolent emperor will rule the world and wars belong to the past. Above all, much of humankind will have paid off their karmic debts and whoever has not reached astral equipoise, will find the opportunity to do so.

Advances in medicine will allow for human life spans in excess of 400 years. For this reason, individuals are granted more time on earth to seek completion of spirit. Ultimately, humans need not incarnate into the physical world anymore since they have become immortal astral beings.

While gaining a better understanding of the workings of positive divine beings, I developed an interest in the negative principle in relation to the cosmic laws. For this reason, I sought out a being that I have known from previous encounters.

To achieve this, I settled into my preferred asana and immediately found myself propelled into a realm of a silky blackness. I noticed a shimmering black light that appeared to be in direct connection with Akasha. Polychrome emanations began shooting off from this light source into the cosmos. The colors appeared to be more saturated and pure than I have experienced in prior encounters with this being of destruction and annihilation. This negative Elohim, together with its millions of subordinates, is in charge of the destruction of entire planets and even suns. Mysterious sounds and vibrations accompanied the streams of lights. Clearly, these vibrations represented destructive Quabbalistic formulas. Nevertheless, purity and wisdom, despite their negative nature, tightly ruled this realm. Even a being of such high standing in the hierarchy, only carries out orders given by Divine Providence. The truth of Akasha being the creating source of this highly destructive being, weighed heavily upon my spirit. At the same time, I had to accept the impeccable purity and divinity of this absolute negative spirit. There are numerous puzzles in this cosmos that may seem to contradict human common sense.

By studying this being, I realized our cosmos' need for having a negative genius for every positive principal genius. This fact presents to humankind the great secret of a cosmic soul mirror (a soul mirror of divine virtues that represent human traits. See: The 1st Lesser Arcanum by J. Hohenstätten). For this reason, every human being must have both, a negative and a positive side of the soul. However, an individual must be in full control of each virtue or attribute, whether positive or negative. The hermetic student will realize that it is necessary to possess equal numbers of positive and negative virtues and traits, just as there are equal numbers of genii and counter genii in our cosmos. This represents the crowning accomplishment of genuine introspection. Through the act of equipoise of all character traits, the truly balanced hermetic imitates the grand (marcrocosmos) within the human soul (microcosmos).

As hermetic practitioners, we will become masters over both, the negative and positive principles, in the same way that the Brethren of Light, the masters of both principles on a cosmic scale, decide over development, wars and other catastrophes. We will realize that the highest principle is the mastery of ALL forces!

Again, I embarked on yet another very profound journey to the highest of all spheres, the so-called "God sphere", while my physical body remained in my room at the spa.

The astral sphere has myriads of degrees of density. Every human being will take his or her place in a plane with a certain degree of subtleness that corresponds to the individual's maturity.

These subtle planes are intensely bright and due to the abstract nature and absence of darkness in the higher planes, human language lacks the complexity to properly describe these planes. Those high planes contain the ideal forms of all religions on earth that represent Akasha or the highest form of God. The foremost Godhead of each religious system dwells in these lofty planes. These Godheads entreat highly evolved humans of faith to incarnate on earth in the capacity of superior initiates. Although, human spirits who dwell in the God spheres, have no need to incarnate. However, out of love and compassion for humankind, these great souls incarnate on earth with a mission.

Once I visited one of these higher planes within the astral sphere and I initially found myself standing in a meadow admits a circle of evergreen oak trees. Immediately, I noticed my guardian spirit standing behind me. He wore a robe that signified the wisdom of a mentor in the astral sphere.

"Where is your God?" said my guardian spirit as I turned towards him.

"My God is in my heart", I replied. "For that reason, he is not present here. My God's realm is in the astral sphere. The Guardian of the Gate assured me that there is no God to be found here in this place.

As you know, I have travelled to the godly realms of Indra, Brahma, and God the Father, Buddha, Allah and the beautiful Shakti and listened to their sweet wisdom, all in search of God. In my mind, I entertained the thought of staying here for all eternity. You are aware of the fact that I may stay, since I have passed the threshold into the lofty planes of light long ago. Nevertheless, I'll return to the coarse physical world to fulfill my mission."

"Yes my son", said my guardian spirit, "and that is the reason, why you are a candidate for additional initiation, beyond the most advanced planes of existence. Even the highest astral levels are perceived coarse and dim relative to the consciousness of supreme beings. Everything in this universe is relative. Behold for what awaits beyond this world of light, as it is much more than you could ever imagine."

My guardian spirit grabbed my right hand while we spiraled upward in a counterclockwise motion through a never-ending spectral burst of polychrome lights, until we ultimately reached a rather dim locale.

Upon my query about the darkness of this place, my

guardian explained that this condition of darkness has been caused by my lack of perception of intense light. However, once my consciousness adjusts to the circumstances, I would be able to utilize my mental visual sense to the fullest extent.

"Here we are neither in the astral nor the mental sphere", my guardian said. "You may have noticed that time exists only in context with your consciousness. It is relative to your present state of mind in regard to the time phenomenon. Hence, since time and space act in accordance, the same principles apply to your sense of space.

This is the sphere, where your eternal self dwells, while the "Brahma Nights" descend upon our world and evolution. You may leave this sphere at will at an instant, but know this: This indescribable sphere holds the indestructible, eternal existence."

As foretold, my mental visual sense began to adapt to the subtle wavelengths of this sphere and I able to capture my surroundings. I began to take notice of the incredible Godhead within my being as the lights reached their zenith of brightness.

"How is it", I asked at the moment the lights began to brighten before my mental eyes, "that no one on earth had ever been spoken of this sphere?"

"This sphere is the exact opposite to earth", my guardian replied. "It may be regarded as most sacred, something beyond description. Behold, Anion, once your mental vision has fully adjusted to this sphere, you shall observe Godheads, who exist in harmonious unity with Divine Providence, while they create new universes and worlds. Through the grace of exalted and illustrious beings, you caught glimpses of such noble events in the past."

Although knowing the answer beforehand, I asked my guardian spirit: "Please tell me, how is it possible that Christ was able to teach his disciples at the same instance as I observed him engaging in creation?"

"Well, that is explained by the phenomenon of omnipresence. As a God, he may accomplish anything at any instance. You too, Anion, will possess this ability one day as well."

I probed further: "My mental body constitutes my existence, my being as an image of God. How can I exist without it?"

"You will not be without a mental body, so to speak, but your mind will exist without form as a formless entity. Since you will attain formlessness, then, in a sense, you will cease to exist. However, you still are! As I stated before, everything is relative. In this state, you have no boundaries. You will have no limits, thus you are omnipresent in every sphere and plane. Now, your matrix, which you have received at the gate of initiation, will demonstrate its true purpose of conflating your spirit conflate with Godhead, without losing your unique consciousness. In the state of formlessness, the mental will adopt the form of your Godhead.

Such cosmic conflation may last millennia. Once concluding a conflation, your spirit will be once more without form. You will become pure energy.

Some religions commonly call this state of existence Nirvana, which means extinction. However, it is the extinction of form, desire, and Samsara. Relative to a being outside this state of existence and plane, the existence within this sphere may be viewed as the discontinuance of all, but this is, in reality, the sphere, where the ultimate existence commences. Once a spirit has established itself here, it will rarely return to the other lower spheres of existence. Due to this, the mistaken idea has evolved that all existence ceases at this point.

The Brethren of Light call this sphere their home. Since some of them incarnate on different occasions, they maintain an astral body through their matrix. A comparison can be found in astral travels where the physical body is preserved through the silver cord.

Human beings that enter this sphere are highly evolved. And there is no requirement to incarnate. No beings here are coerced by divine will. Every spirit is free to do anything. It is the sphere, where humans cease to be human and for that reason, initiates call this sphere the divine sphere. The divine sphere is and always will be sparsely populated, since most human beings decide to dissolve into the divine light after concluding their paths."

"Why are you showing me a world, from which I am a long way removed", I asked my guardian.

"See it as a blessing or a curse", my guardian responded. "You must not dissolve into the divine light, and since you have become tired of life, you shall be permitted a glimpse into the future. There are good reasons, why you were permitted to encounter some of the Godheads of the godly spheres. You were unaware of the causes, and you shall be enlightened. However, bear in mind to rid yourself of all self-destructive thoughts. You don't want to anger Divine Providence!"

Meanwhile, I was able to catch a glimpse when my Godhead assumed forms that I had not known previously. Here I humbly stood, outside my mental form, before a God, when my guardian spirit pulled me back into my mental body, a body that would have been far too coarse to reach the heights of this "God sphere".

With a weary and perturbed mind, I retired upon a rock in that initial meadow from whence I started my journey, to gather my thoughts. Thousands upon thousands of thoughts flashed and bounced through my mind, while I was trying to bring order to my thought processes.

Once I had returned to my physical body, I decided to terminate my spa stay, partly due to the news of my wife's health condition and due to depression over the fact that I would have to proceed with my present incarnation. For some time I entertained the thought of entering the astral sphere permanently. Alas, now I have been tasked to remain and continue life in the physical world a while longer. Once more, the physical world held me in her clutches.

At home, I meditated extensively over my experiences in the spiritual realms and my encounters with my guardian spirit. I raised the question: Who was this godly spirit that guided me through life? How did he acquire all his knowledge and wisdom?

A guardian spirit is always watching over his protégé and gives aid to spiritual and physical matters. Usually, the guardian spirit operates from the astral sphere, although it may happen that a guardian spirit incarnates near his protégé. Such incarnations are purely on a voluntary basis and may occur, when a group of hermetic seekers incarnates simultaneously, and should such a guardian pass away, one of the guardian spirit's subordinates will take on the task.

There are high-ranking guardian spirits, who have never been incarnated. Such spirits guide advanced seekers on their path. Other guardian spirits are advanced humans that passed over from the physical realm upon death, who want to eradicate some remaining karma by helping others in life.

Since my last journey with my guardian spirit, the God sphere enraptured my entire being. Before this visit, I was studying the Mercury sphere, but now, I have now come to the realization that this God sphere had some analogies to our earth. Only traces of all four elements are present in the God sphere. However, the electric and magnetic fluids are part of this sphere's make-up in a most subtle way. Space and time only play a role relative to the perception of an individual visiting this sphere, as there are no space-time concepts in the overall structure of the God sphere. I pondered many hours over all the newly discovered laws and circumstances in the God sphere. All this lead to a new thought that gained prominence in my mind: How is a macrocosm created?

"In all those centuries, your brazenness has not subsided", my guardian spirit sneered in my mind's ear. "However, I can understand your desire to educate your students. Most of them will reach this sphere, so they should know in advance."

As instructed by my guardian spirit, I assumed my asana

and concentrated on my mental body separation. Within a moment after the separation, I stood before a great spiritual being, whose name I am not permitted to reveal. However, this being stands in direct contact with Divine Providence.

I first noticed some fine, yet powerful energy flowing into the being. Initially this energy appeared barely noticeable, but soon a magic volt with an electric inner and a magnetic outer charge forcefully expanded from this being far into the cosmos.

As the magnetic force seemed to increase, the volt, which formed into a huge sphere, began to oscillate and burst into the elements of fire and water. Once a perfect sun had formed, a lightning ray of Akasha burst into the sun's center. Akasha swiftly eclipsed this new sun and the sound *"ÄÄÄ"* (ä sounds similar to the "a" in "lack") reverberated from within its core. Gradually, the sun began to shine with a beautiful brightness that almost blinded my mental eyes.

Dust that formed into planets began to separate from this Akashic sun and the sound *"MÖ-MÖ-MÖ"* resonated through the entire system.

A supreme being, which stood in close communion with Divine Providence, had become a creator. Omniconsciousness permeated every particle of his creation. Genii and counter-genii, an entire hierarchy of principals sprang forth from the supreme being's Akashic principle, while they received their duties and missions from Providence. All ten Quabbalistic keys were spoken.

Now, this Supreme Being created mental, astral and physical conditions by utilizing complex Quabbalistic formulas. Much to my amazement, I immediately began to feel the concepts of time and space around me, as I gazed at the wonders of creation.

Then, within an instant, Akasha obscured the sun that has become Metatron. This occultation of light demonstrated the might of Metatron, in whom even light bows in reverence.

Gradually, the Light-Brother awoke from his trance into an indescribable outpour of eternal joy

"How far are we removed from the earth in physical terms?" I casually asked my guide.

"Not an easy question", my guardian spirit replied. He closed his eyes for a moment and then said: "about 700 light years in physical terms."

Gripped with fascination and awe, I inspected this newly made macrocosm, whose light will reach our earth in 700 years.

19.

Previous Incarnations

Before I will recount some of my past incarnations, I would want to illustrate some of my experiences within the demonic realms that I had gathered, due to a pact I sealed with a high-ranking negative being.

Some hundreds of years in the past, I had sealed a pact with a demonic being, and as a result, I enjoyed many advantages in material life. Alas, a dependence upon this being rapidly increased until the end.

While dying, I convinced myself that even a demon being is part and parcel of Divine Providence, and a pact with such a being would not violate any karmic laws. Although a negative path may lead to Divine Providence, it is not a path meant for human beings to tread, since humans are by nature more divine that any demon of any rank or standing.

Once I separated from my physical shell, I awoke in the realm of this demon. This realm's surreal environment aroused the impression of a genuinely horrific a nightmare. An ever-present stench of burning sulfur, and jagged, sharp pulsating lights that stirred my soul, underlined the grotesque environment in which I now lived.

From this moment onward, I had become a servant to a demon, whose responsibility included the infliction of horrible and devastating human diseases.

"I am your God now", said demon as I stood before his throne, "I shall take your conscience from you. Through my influence, you will soon adjust to your surroundings and all ghastly tasks beforehand. Your old identity shall be forgotten and never mentioned under the threat of punishment, as long as you shall serve my interests. Your demonic name, henceforth, shall be GANUS."

Once he spoke those words he vanished, leaving two female subordinates, who initiated me into their Gods properties.

"When the occasion arises that human beings have to be taught by karma", one of the females said, "our master will burden such individuals with certain diseases, and if necessary, such burdens will linger until death and beyond. We are given some liberty, as to what disease and its degree of severity will serve the purpose."

Soon I felt quite comfortable in my new surroundings. My new master became my mentor and I began enjoying my work. I became proficient and conscientiously fulfilled my tasks. From time to time, my master rewarded me with promotions and further initiations into my master demon's path. After 70 earth years I, had become Lord Ganus and counted more than 200 subordinates. Being an enthusiastic student, I learned how various diseases originated, and what karmic implications they served.

However, there were instances, when my conscience began to break through the hard shell that surrounded my divine spark, to remind me of my human nature. On many occasions, I silenced any conscience by becoming convinced that I could actually heal diseases by inverting the steps that cause disease from within the demonic sphere.

One day, my master announced that I had served all my time in his realm; my pact had expired. Although, he wished that I stayed beyond my pact's span. He offered promotions to the rank of a prince with a thousand subordinates at my disposal.

His offer was tempting, especially since I could learn more practices. However, I knew that if I had stayed, I would have lost all human traits. The price of staying was too high.

Reluctantly, my master released me with the words: "If you would stay, I would elevate you to unimaginable heights with seemingly limitless powers."

"I served you well", I responded, "but now, our contract has expired and just as you had ordered me to your realm upon my bodily death, my true God is calling me back. Therefore, my decision is final."

I respectfully bowed before my former master one last time and soon after I rose upwards to my rightful astral level, where I felt free and light, a feeling that I had forgotten a long time ago.

My guardian spirit stood before me with tears of joy in his eyes and welcomed me like a long lost son. He did not say anything, uttered no reproach. Just silence. In this savoring silence, I enjoyed being human again and made a promise to my guardian that I will heal whomever God will allow me to heal.

"Please help me to find a new incarnation", I begged my guardian spirit, "so that I can continue my development and strengthen my character."

My guardian conceded and promised an arduous incarnation in India, where I ought to follow the path of yoga in order to relearn all human values anew.

This incarnation in India gave me the opportunity to utilize the skills I obtained in the demonic sphere towards constructive purposes. Through a strict yoga teacher, I had elevated my spiritual understanding beyond the level of my life in the demonic realm. Gradually, I began healing many maladies. Although my former master, the demonic principal, did not appreciate the use of skills I obtained under his tutelage, for constructive purposes., he had no jurisdiction over my life on earth anymore. To this day, I honed the skills of healing and I will heal and help wherever possible until my dying days.

In another incarnation, two lifetimes ago, I had been living in Tibet. My master and mentor at a monastery there, is my guardian spirit to this day He stands at my side at times of need and advise me whenever necessary. By signing a pact with a demon prince in a past lifetime, I had deeply insulted and hurt my guardian.

Even though I displayed certain abilities, I was not seen as a model pupil. My talents saved me from dismissal from the monastery. Furthermore, my guardian also took my predicament of being placed under the influence of a demon into account, which explained some of my excessive behavior.

In any case, I had access to the universal path up to what could be similar to *Step III* in Bardon's first book. Later in life, I vowed to continue with magic, even if I would be unsuccessful to advance.

Throughout my life in Tibet, fate tested the metal of my vow on numerous occasions. However, I found success and my vow became my blessing. In the end, I understood the meaning and implications of a pledge, promise or oath towards God and the grave consequences of a broken pledge.

Eventually, I was initiated in the most important part of hermetic training that a Magus could wish to discover, namely true humanity. Such a God-given gift is rare and few of the noblest and virtuous human beings were bestowed with the great honor to receive this gift. Many of these noble individuals never practiced the hermetic teachings and in spite of this lack of schooling, they proved to be of a more noble character that some hermetic practitioners, who had been walking the path for many years. Above all, individuals of such magnanimous humanity instilled into their character, do not diverge from their path, despite adversity.

On the negative side, there are many people who act selfishly and covetous. Those poor "devils" are held captive on the lowly spheres by their own character traits. These wretched souls deserve all our sympathies.

Once I lived out my life, I passed on to the astral sphere, where I had the opportunity to choose an incarnation with another mentor, who also became my earthly father in Sweden.

In Sweden, my father and spiritual mentor was the head of a secret Rosicrucian order. Both parents initiated me in secret exercises, meditations and rites. My mother was a kind and strong woman who also taught me true humanity.

Upon my father's death, it was my mother's wish that I took my father's post as the head of the Rosicrucian society. I remained in this position for many years. Within this society of noble Rosicrucians, I furthered my knowledge and wisdom. Once I passed away at a ripe age, I realized what absolute freedom was bestowed upon me in the astral sphere. My father was a high-ranking magus there. Eventually, I contacted some of the Brethren of Light.

On one occasion, the coming of a cosmic master was announced. Every being in this part of the astral world had some knowledge of this master, whose astral achievements were familiar to all.

Master Arion's invited us a gathering at a round table. All of us rejoiced at the appearance of the master and with great anticipation as we glanced at a throne-like chair on with master began to materialize astrally. Gradually, Master Arion took form. His aura emanated a bright blue light as he sat among us. Forthwith, Master Arion taught profound spiritual truths that were obscured to us before his arrival. After he spoke his final concluding words to the group, and while I was in the process to leave, the master gestured for me to stay and spoke: "In the near future, I will reveal the first three Tarot Cards to the material world, regardless of the fact that they originally to be issued at a later time in the

27th century. Naturally, for this very reason, the books will be published on earth prematurely at a precarious time. I am engaging you for support to help guide chosen neophytes on their path. The preoccupation with the material world at this time will be against them in their spiritual endeavors.

You may utilize your magical abilities wherever necessary, and you may give the students that open themselves to you even more than that. Accordingly, one of my acolytes should incarnate in Greece."

Although, my Greek counterpart was of a higher spiritual rank than I, Arion would stand by my side, should I need assistance due to some peculiar karma I had to work on.

I was instructed to incarnate in Germany, where I was to master "Initiation into Hermetics" within 9 months and once I turned 20 years of age, I was told to be teaching others. In this incarnation, I chose a difficult father to condition my will and develop the strength I needed in order to teach spiritual subtleties in the harsh realities of a material world.

Diligently I supervised my students in this present incarnation, while I was personally working on evocations. I also began to write books to supplement the hermetic writings of Master Arion. One of my books included the 4th Tarot Card.

I stretched my karma to the limit by writing the 1st Lesser Arcanum. However, Providence did not intervene in order to hinder the book's completion. In previous times, a master gave this Lesser Arcanum to his student in the astral sphere. This knowledge may become dangerous to the practitioner, who abuses it for more egotistical purposes.

Throughout my life, I practiced magical evocation. Consequently, my favorite student will perceive my true depth of spirit once he had matured. Above all, he will evoke spirits in the end and wander through spheres that seem unreal to the untrained mind.

One task I regarded as particularly difficult to execute proved to be the interpretation of the 72 names of God. Alas, there are no detailed sources in Western writings pertaining to these 72 names of God. However, I found help through a mercurial genius named Lehlahel. He also drew to my attention that all 72 mercurial genii carry the syllable "ah" and "el" in their names. "Ah" stands for: "You have gained consciousness." he "el" stands for: "Virtue realized in the purest light."

I was in the position to complete this little book about the 72 names of God only with Lehlahel's assistance. The verses in the book present much potential power since they are considered mantrams that lead to a union of diverse divine conceptions. The experienced mantric practitioner can experience almost all concepts of God through these verses that, when combined, make up the longest name of God, the Shemhamphorasch.

Furthermore, I decided that the art of Rune Magick did not deserve to be forgotten or be falsely interpreted by many of today's rune authors. Since practitioners will realize that there is a close relationship between Rune Magick and Quabbalah, it is understandable that both practices share all the same powers and efficaciousness. Judging from my own experiences, I found Rune Magick quite effective. However, there is one caveat: Rune Magick may be quite dangerous if not practiced diligently and without the slightest oversight. It should be practiced only with the tutelage of an experienced master druid.

Presently, I am working on the 5th Tarot Card. Although, my enthusiasm for alchemy is limited, I fulfilled my mission accordingly. The 4th Card, the card of wisdom was written compendiously, due to the tradition that the student uses the words as a guide to spur the reader's imagination and intuition.

My counterpart in Greece once told me that he does not write anything due to the nature of his unique mission. He is well known as a healer far beyond his village. I prefer my relative anonymity. This way I have more time for my students and my writings.

As mentioned before, I consider my students as my mission, and it is my goal that at least seven of the 14 reach the higher portals of development. I will use my abilities and skills to guide them on their way. Furthermore, I commissioned some genii from different spheres to protect and guide my protégées in the way of intuition and inspiration, preventing them from harm and major diseases and strengthen the bonds between my students and their respective guardian spirits. However, the ones that lead astray from the path must fend for themselves. Albeit, I see my students quite infrequent to keep my students from developing a dependency, a situation that can karmically viewed as of a pact. By the same token, I will be here when my "children" need me.

Admittedly, there were disagreements with demons of different ranks and positions about my actions and interactions with my students. In the end, however, all these genii had to accept my approach. For this reason, I will never deny my assistance. Only my physical death may hinder me in some way, but never completely, since I will be there astrally and guide my students toward the light of realization

With this in mind, I possess abundant eternal fervor, on which I shall delight myself.

Book II

My Hermetic World

1.

Demonology

The Realms of the Demons

This chapter poses a brief introduction to some arch-demons that rule the material world. The neophyte should know that a direct contact with any of the arch-demons will lead to certain death, unless such a hermetic student has advanced far enough to have achieved absolute union with his Godhead. Besides the below described arch-demons, there are many more within the hierarchy of supra-genii.

Without the arch-demons that are the rightful rulers of the material world, the existence of the material plane would have not been possible. The material plane can be regarded as the adversary of the mental plane.

There is not any comfort in the idea that according to the hierarchy, two of the below mentioned arch-demons are Elohim, or in other words, they are creative Godheads. These demon Gods are tetra-polar, hence they are immortal. Furthermore, they were created as beings of purity that rule over the principles of obliteration or destruction. All below mentioned demons are supreme divine beings, whose minds are far beyond the comprehension of ordinary humans.

Naturally, the principle of obliteration, destruction and hardship must be viewed as a part of evolution; hence the negative principle must be considered a divine virtue. The student of hermetics will now understand that the balanced path of the golden means is the perfect universal way to develop spiritually.

Once an individual becomes a sphere magus, he must also contact the negative genii and the principals of the negative cosmic hierarchy, or face a one-sided development. The rhythm of all life in all spheres depends on opposing poles of positive and negative, active and passive, light and dark. I experienced many ups and downs, and good and evil, throughout my various incarnations and have seen inconceivable abysmal chasms. Then again, I have likewise seen lofty transcendental heights that very few can imagine: to summarize, my cognizance is my bliss.

Much could be added to the short descriptions of these Elohim. However, a brief account of the basic character and missions of these arch-demons should suffice. In order to avoid misuse, and for the sake of the safety for the reader, I have omitted the sigils of these arch-demons.

Satan

In the beginning of creation, before our solar system formed, this arch-demon demanded free will, independence in judgment, free action and responsibility. Satan is the master of the astral light and all negative genii. The seven biblical deadly sins were bestowed upon humankind by this Godhead. While dipping his hands into chaos (Akasha) and uttering Quabbalistic formulae, he created the planet earth. Through the densification of chaos our planet formed and took its place in our solar system. Satan's creation of earth was the result of defiance, since he was to have his free will denied. For this, he was marooned into the material realm, a circumstance that limits his activities. For this reason, earth is a peculiar planet. Initially, earth should not have come here into existence. The reason the planet exists, remains a secret found within Divine.

Satan is simultaneously God and man, and also the foremost prince ruler of earth. Once marooned on earth, Satan remains as an incorporeal spirit and he existed prior to humankind's creation. One of his peculiar traits is that he is a hermaphrodite who came forth from Akasha together with all other negative beings in our cosmos. Human development made it necessary for Satan being the snake in Paradise at the same time, when the snake is also the bringer of knowledge and in a world, where negative and positive forces coexist, knowledge can be readily misused.

Lucifer

This arch-demon embodies the spirit of intellectual

enlightenment and free thought. Lucifer's highest aspect of is that of an enlightened Godhead, and the lower aspect is that of is that of a nemesis. Both aspects are reflected in the human spirit. Lucifer is the first brother of Satan and just like all other arch-demons, his sphere of influence is the material world and the material aspect of the macrocosm.

Baphomet

As the creator of the magnum opus (life) and the astral light, the oldest form of light, Baphomet embodies the one who has separated from God. On earth, the astral light is known as the life force or prana. Everything that exists came forth from prana. Baphomet inspired early man to invent the first weapons and the magic mirrors, which were used in the annihilation of adversaries. Baphomet attains his power by feeding on the higher and lower realms and he acts as the ambassador of God's words of wisdom. However, he became the scapegoat because he created women as a negative principle. He and all other arch-demons act macrocosmically in the material and lower astral realms. All acts of the arch-demons and their subordinates are a necessary part of evolution. If the negative principle would seize, nothing that is positive could flourish.

Samael

Samael is considered to be identical to Jehovah. This

arch-demon is a spirit of earth and one of the seven Elohim. Symbolically, Samael represents Saturn or Kronos, the son of Uranus. Jehovah and Saturn are identical in a cryptic sense. Moreover, in Jewish Kabbalah, Samael and Michael, the slayer of the dragon, are considered indistinguishable. He was given the task of misguidance of humankind and initiated the biblical Fall of Man. However, Samael embodies hidden wisdom, whereas Michael embodies higher earthly wisdom, although both originated from the same Divine Providence. Samael's mission includes the process of human development and perfection. Owning to his distaste of nature, Samael prefers lifeless deserts.

Baal

Baal, a Sun God and the Creator of deceit, may awaken the dead, should he draw advantages from such endeavors. He personifies and manifests the primal concept of darkness. Although his reign is limitless, he disguises himself as a lowly being at times. In times immemorial, he split the universal language into many individual tongues. This arch-demon bears the mark of impurity. Baal, as the all-devouring fire, destroys life force at his whim. A sphere magus who contacts this arch-demon may gain great wisdom, but lo and behold, Baal also epitomizes amnesia. Naturally, within his sphere of influence are all venoms and toxic substances discovered in plants, mushrooms, snakes and insects. He inspires humankind to devise and create all sorts of poisonous formulae. Any mistake carried out in the preparation of conjuring this arch-demon or any omission of precautions may prove deadly not only physically, but mentally as well. Baal epitomizes devaluation.

2.

The Beings of the Elements

Sexuality, like in the physical world, does exist in all elemental realms, since all four elements and their realms are closely related to the physical world. However, in the astral sphere proper, sexuality has no function or purpose. The elemental realm, although being a part of the astral sphere, its density relates to the physical planet earth and its biological functions. For this reason, one will encounter children of both sexes in all the realms of the elements.

Salamanders: The Beings of the Fire Element

Despite that fact that I have seen and experienced much while traveling the realms, my first conscious encounter with a prince of the fire element stirred much astonishment. A fire being, in its primeval form, cannot even be categorized as a being with proper forms and proportions, but rather a light source with an enormous radiance that affects one's mental body. Despite the fact that the mental body does not capture feelings and emotions well — the astral body incorporates all the feelings — I felt the charges of electricity within my mental self. The onslaught of the fiery fluids hindered my thought process, diminished my will and my ability to take action. Needless to say, it took several attempts to establish a successful contact with this fiery prince. Of all elemental beings, Salamanders, male and female, are generally most unlike human beings in appearance.

Eventually, the source of light that embodied the being I encountered, formed into a long, slender ray that gradually lost its intensity. And the fire prince took a faintly recognizable human form that moved to and fro nervously and disquietingly, assuming ever-changing shapes. The being's face was elongated with a strict and grave expression. Its elongated neck had thrice the length of its human counterpart. Overall, Salamanders of all ranks are much taller than humans. In appearance, Salamanders of higher ranks have more similarities to humans that the lower fire spirits. During my encounter, I had great difficulties to emulate the Salamander's shape mentally. While communicating with beings of the fire element, the hermetic practitioner must mobilize his utmost powers of mental imagination to fixate a being that constantly shifts its shape. The Salamander would not have recognized and noticed me, had I failed to emulate the appearance of a proper Salamander. The being I encountered, never stood still and constantly flickered like a flame in the wind. Eventually, the fire being addressed me with a shrill voice and asked what I desired. I stated my wish to learn to control the electric fluid as the reason for having entered his realm.

Eventually, the Salamander and I began engaging in conversation. Being of a higher rank, this Salamander prince revealed a nimble mind and keen intelligence. Through his guidance, I absorbed numerous secrets he divulged about his element. I learned about various applications of using the electric fluid and countless methods of healing through the fire element.

Gradually, a relationship of mutual sympathy developed and I did not sense the disturbing radiance that I felt during our initial encounter. The Salamander prince diligently explained the process of fluid condensers and he promised that one of his subservient spirits would assist me with the process of charging condensers. Furthermore, I was initiated into the dry and hot path of alchemy.

At numerous occasions, the Salamander prince advised against the process of evocation as a means of contact, I would have had to charge the room with concentrated fire element during the preparations. Such concentrated charges of the fire element could ignite the evocation-magus's surroundings in an instant. Then he told me of cases where entire families perished in instantly combusting fires, while the entire house burned to its foundation in an explosive sea of flames.

This particular Salamander has been described in Franz Bardon's book *The Practice of Magic Evocation* as a being that has a difficult disposition. However, after initial hurdles, a friendship emerged and I am still visiting him from time to time. At occasions, this Salamander even visited me in my dreams, where he explained the dream symbolism of the fire element.

The Salamanders, should they not appear in abstract form, are clothed, but the sun-like radiance of the beings makes details of dress impossible to discern. Salamanders of noble rank, such as emperors and princes, wear crowns that symbolize their rank and standing.

During my visits to the realm of fire, I have seen barren, rocky and mountainous landscapes throughout this realm. Although, some stunted plant growth, no taller than three feet (1m) in height, sparsely dotted the environment.

Furthermore, I noticed some form of buildings that only remotely resemble buildings here in our world. Owning to their abstract nature, I have difficulties describing them. Furthermore, I saw animals. Again, they do not resemble anything on earth. This fire plane also exhibits gigantic storms that could cause harm to an individual's astral body. However, a magus's mental body has proven to be immune to injury from such storms.

For the common fire beings, these storms pose some sort of nourishment. Otherwise, the element itself nourishes the Salamanders with vital life force. Just as it is common in all spiritual realms, the beings here communicate telepathically. Generally, the more subtle parts of the fiery sphere are flooded by a glaring brightness. The lower regions appear in a saturated yellow light.

The mental body proves to be quite tolerant of the oscillations of the fiery element. Only an encounter with a Salamander may cause initial mental discomfort.

Therefore, an adept is advised not to visit this sphere in astral form until perfect equipoise is achieved or the adept has shed the earthly shell permanently. Although, visiting the fiery sphere without seeking Salamanders, poses no danger to the health of the adept.

Undines: The Beings of the Water Element

The oscillations of the water element have a much more serene effect on an adept visiting this realm, in comparison to visits to the realms of the fire element. Generally, Undines are very gregarious and a visiting adept may encounter Undines after only one or two visits. The adept will observe that Undines possess a human form, unlike the mermaids in fairy tales, paintings and illustrations who show the lower body of those beings with a fish tail. Only during evocations do the Undines manifest a fish tail as a symbol of their element. It is up to the evocating adept's discretion whether the being appeared with a tail or human legs.

The extraordinary power of attraction that Undines of both sexes exhibit may easily discombobulate a visiting adept's consciousness. This disturbance within one's consciousness poses a danger when consorting with Undines. Master Arion has mentioned these dangers multiple times in his works.

Once a water being acknowledged the adept, he should request an audience with a higher-ranking Undine in order to avoid disciplinary actions taken against a lower ranking being by its superiors for unauthorized contact.

Here in the water element plane, a higher the rank of an Undine translates into a greater spiritual beauty and force of attraction. At the first moment of my encounter with a superior Undine, I realized the danger of seduction, thus losing authority over my own will power. Her radiance, due to her mastery of the magnetic fluid, disrupted my consciousness to the point of incapacitation. With a voice, lovely and sensual, yet clear and eloquent, she wondered how she might serve me. At this instant, I became aware of my perilous situation. Eventually, this lovely, most beautiful Undine would ensnare my soul and my path would conclude in this sphere. With all the willpower I could muster, I requested a meeting with a male Undine, although, even a male Undine is equipped with such amount of magnetism that they arouse homosexual desires even in heterosexual males. Fortunately, no such feelings arose during my encounter, but I must warn any future adept that even the seductive male Undines may pose danger male adepts.

This male being that I contacted was friendly and respectful. Although we spoke about general things concerning the water element, he most importantly broached unknown and secret aspects of his element. For example, he told me that the sun influences all water beings and once they reached the end of their life span, Undines merge into the water principle aspect of Metatron. Moreover, this male water being conveyed the fact that without the sun sphere and the physical sun, the water element could not exist. In addition, he taught me healing methods for body, soul and spirit and revealed how to use any water surface to foretell the future and other secrets about the constructive and destructive magnetic forces that I am not at liberty to divulge.

The water sphere radiates an abundance of fertility. There are lush tall trees and beautiful meadows, luxuriant with flowers and other greenery. High-ranking Undines live in castles that are similar to the ones described in fairy tales. Even common houses are ornate and adorned with artistry of stunning beauty. Multiple times, I was a guest at one of these houses. All rooms were decorated with wonderful crystals that were emitting light. Tables and chairs had a glassy appearance and many walls are constructed of mirrors that can be utilized to communicate with the physical world.

The emperors and empresses are found in the major oceans of the world. Princes and princesses rule over large rivers and big lakes. Lower ranking Undines care for small rivers, lakes, brooks and ponds. Generally, positive beings are found in clean and unpolluted water, whereas sewer and highly polluted waters are part of the realm of negative Undines (even polluted parts of the oceans and seas). I was reproached by Undines in many instances of extreme pollution of water human hand; even the highest ranked Undines were incapable of mending the waters' conditions with all their magical powers. In some instances, the water element aspect of Divine Providence had to intervene, in order to initiate harmony in such waters.

Positive Undines are strangers to avarice and greed. However, the negative Undines are quite exultant to acquire new territories in polluted waters. For example, the Ganges River presents a sad example of a place where negative Undines comfortably dwell.

In one instance, I had an Undine guide me to the frontiers of the negative realm of the water element, in order to enter into this realm. There, I came upon unimaginably odious and foul bodies of water. The ever-present stench in those ghastly realms gnaws unceasingly upon one's consciousness. All the beings here are unsightly and ugly and display a wily and wretched character. I declined to visit any high ranking being in this part of the water realm.

Once back in my physical body, I changed my ways, stopped using toxic materials and attempted to heal and nurse creeks and small lakes nearby where I lived. All this caused friction and resentment from people living in this area. These individuals had no idea what they were doing. The proverb "ignorance is bliss" is incorrect. Ignorance does not save an individual from karma accrued by misdeeds perpetrated in ignorance.

Sylphs: The Beings of the Air Element

The Sylphs are similar to humans in shape and form, although their skin has a slightly blue complexion. There are some highly attractive female Sylphs in this realm. Generally, all Sylphs are very reserved towards humans. With the event of global air pollution, beginning with the industrial revolution, these beings have become even more reserved and resentful towards humans and fancy no contact with us.

The adept does not have to change the mental body's shape before entering the realm of the air element. Although I recommend a concentration of air element within the mental body, before visiting this realm, as it facilitates contact with Sylphs. It took me 5 months worth of routine visits, until a Sylph contacted me. This particular Sylph was very unfriendly, but I detected some sympathies toward humans in his heart. This Sylph radiated dignity and grace, usually found in higher-ranking Sylphs, regardless of the fact that he was by no means an emperor or a prince. Similar to Salamanders, the air beings are jittery and restless just like the air is always in motion in our earth's atmosphere.

My contact had the rank of a lord with many subordinates at his disposal. He appeared in a white gown, woven of a material similar to silk. This lord taught me about the passive process of the electromagnetic fluid and its practical application. When I say passive, I do not mean negative, because air is the mediator element between water and fire. It is a buffer zone between the two poles. Fire reaches into air from one side and water on the other side. My Sylph contact also taught me the great mystery of the electromagnetic fluid with respect to the air element. The passive electromagnetic fluid is an especially superior force that is generally unknown. Only initiates are skilled in the way to apply the passive electromagnetic fluid. Higher ranked Sylphs are gifted alchemists. Unfortunately, they are very reluctant to divulge their secrets and only after some time, my Sylph friend willingly divulged other mysteries. Through his mediation, I hope to be able to contact an emperor of the air element in the near future. Such a superior being is difficult to control, because he possesses great powers, which he utilizes to form storms, tornadoes and hurricanes. One might interject that storms such as hurricanes are negative, e.g. destructive, in nature. From the anthropological aspect on earth, such weather patterns may appear destructive and negative, but examined holistically, and adept will recognize the healing power of such weather formations to our atmosphere.

The realm of the air element is variable and ever changing and shifting. However there are dwellings that vaguely resemble buildings with ever-changing appearances. Emperors rule in large, ever-changing palaces. During one of my visits, I also noticed plant life, which I am unable to describe due to their strictly abstract nature. These plants manifest in our physical world in plants that aid in the breathing process, such as the peppermint, lungwort, oregano or the eucalyptus tree, etc.

Gnomes: The Beings of the Earth Element

The earth element is the densest of all four elemental realms in the astral sphere. The adept will be able to assimilate to the shape of a Gnome with ease. The visitor to this realm only needs to shrink the mental body in size and cumulate the earth element mentally. As always, the adept must charge the mental body with the element specific to the corresponding plane, before any visit. Otherwise, he would be invisible to the beings of the elemental planes.

The realm of the Gnomes is not so perilous as the water and fire realms. Gnomes are friendly and talkative creatures. Therefore, making contact is relatively easy. Gnomes' nature is amicable and they are quite sympathetic towards humans. Their character is opposite to that of the Sylphs. In this realm, as in all the others, emperors live in palaces — in this case underground palaces — and subordinates of lower ranks dwell in smaller structures. That is one of the universal laws, which not only applies to the elemental realms and the zone girdling the earth, but ultimately to all spheres.

Before entering the earth element realm, I had chosen a Gnome emperor I wanted to visit. The first contact had transpired quickly. This particular emperor initially appeared somewhat arrogant, but eventually, he turned out to be kind and very generous. For example, he allocated two of is subordinates as my aides. The Gnome king temporarily transplanted his own faculties into these two subordinates for the time that they were to serve me. One of the subordinates was a real comedian. He also gave me his permission to photograph him in the magic mirror. I still have the picture in my possession.

This emperor was somewhat smaller in height, at about 1.5 meters (5 feet) in height. In the Gnome empire, rank is directly proportional to a being's height. Some subordinates may only reach the height of 10 centimeters (4 inches). The adept is recommended to adjust the size of the mental body to be somewhat larger in comparison to the Gnome emperor that the adept wishes to visit. It is a universal law that sizes matters in this realm, as it symbolizes rank and order.. The adept will research the size of the respective Gnome empire beforehand through transcendental sight to aid the size adjustment.

The emperor and I discussed alchemy and healing methods through the earth element. At that time, he mentioned the fact that, should karma permit it, I may be involved in the field of healthcare. He was an accomplished mind reader. It is apparent that the beings of the earth element are the most accomplished mind readers of all the beings of the other elements. During one of the audiences with the Gnome king, I petitioned him to evoke a small amount of the Red Lion into a physical vessel. He concurred under the condition that I shall never take advantage of the stone unless most severe maladies necessitate its use. I was present while the Gnome king created the stone. The creation was accomplished by using water-soluble salts and crystalline dust in an unconventional distillery apparatus. To a casual observer, the process may appear simple, but the various oscillations of rays that emanated from the Gnome king into the stone made it clear that a degree of complexity and mental discipline was involved in the creative process.

During this process, the material transformed semblance and color at numerous occasions. I assumed that this emperor was an accomplished quabbalist, a skill I never expected from an elemental being.

Overall, the earth realm appears darker than the other spheres I have visited. Strange small trees and other growth of crystalline appearance and texture flourish in a realm that is absent of bright light. In general, sources of light contribute to less radiance and luster, when compared to the other three realms.

Of all the other three elemental realms, the earth realm relates more directly to our physical world, due to the density and character of the earth element. For this reason, some children and mediumistic individuals may encounter Gnomes that have come to our world to collect plants or other materials, which they utilize in alchemistic processes. Since these harvester Gnomes are of lower ranks, they may have neglected to maintain their stealth owing to their lack of attentiveness and intelligence.

Naturally, there are female Gnomes who are quite beautiful, contrary to some illustrations published in past times. Although they lack the attraction of Undines, the beauty of female Gnomes far surpasses the beauty of their human female counterparts.

Describing the sphere of the earth element in its entirety would pose a daunting task and would fill two large volumes. Even such volumes would just touch upon the basic description. There are so many issues to consider such as chemical reactions, organic and inorganic matter, and crystallization, etc. that would be outside the scope of this work. I hope that the reader has gained more insights into the elemental realms through my brief descriptions of my experiences in these realms.

3.

The Extra-Cosmic Planets

Uranus

As a planet, Uranus has 14.5 times the mass of earth. It radiates 1.06 times the energy that it receives from the sun, which is less than the energy radiation of the other Jovian planets. However, only the astral plane of the Uranus sphere is of major interest to the adept.

There are 48 primal genii whose powers are quite limitless and abstract in nature. Upon the completion of creation, Metatron placed the entire set of Quabbalistic keys into the hands of these genii. Therefore, the Uranus sphere represents the cosmic language.

The Uranus sphere is considered the higher octave of the Mercury sphere's oscillations. Therefore, the adept who visits this sphere will detect a relationship of Uranus' oscillations and the mental body. However, in the Uranus sphere, the adept's spirit will transform into an ultra-spirit and work is performed predominantly on a macrocosmic level, serving as a creative Godhead. The difference between Metatron and the adept's spirit are miniscule once the Uranus sphere has been mastered.

Neptune

Bardon omitted this planet's sphere completely from his book for a good reason: Neptune is the higher octave of Venus. One can only speculate, what kind of attractive force dominates the Neptune sphere. It is needless to say that the female genii of this sphere are of indescribable divine beauty that can paralyze the senses of any adept, except those of the highest ranks. This sphere can pose a real danger even to far advanced adepts. The sheer unimaginable beauty of beings, their attractive magnetism, and their surroundings are outside the scope of even the most gifted artistic imagery.

Neptune is the manifestation of perfect seduction, to which Venus and its genii pale in comparison. Sadly, some of the inhabitants of the Neptune sphere are highly evolved magus, who surrendered their development. Almost God-like, these sad examples of adepts spiraled down from their lofty spiritual position to mere sensuality.

However, an adept who has mastered and overcome the seductive perils of the Neptune sphere will receive theurgic powers and become a master of divine love.

Although I am in possession of the sigils of the Neptunian genii, I will not divulge any details about their design. Anyone shall heed the image of Neptune clutching his trident as a symbol of mastery of the divine aspect of the water element.

Pluto

At first I was reluctant to write about this planet and its sphere, but the importance of the subject matter outweighed my initial misgivings.

In Greek mythology, Pluto is the God of the underworld. In earlier times, he was otherwise known as Hades, the name of the underworld itself. Although, mythology gave Pluto a more positive image as a ruler of the underworld, his character is generally negative in the hermetic sense.

Pluto is the annihilator of all life. In cosmic hierarchy, Pluto is considered furthest from the sun. Thus, Pluto represents the antagonist of the sun or Metatron.

At this time, the Pluto sphere has no influence in our evolutionary cycle, even though Pluto crosses Neptune's orbit.

Altogether, the Plutonian genii are of a quite demonic nature. Even the supposedly positive genii are a 1000-fold more dangerous that their Martian counterparts, since Pluto represents the higher octave of Mars.

Entering the Plutonian sphere would spell immediate mental death to an unprepared adept, who has not mastered the Uranus sphere and utilized its protective formulae.

Once, in a distant future, a war shall be conducted between the sun and Pluto. However, the sun shall be victorious, not because it is physically bigger, but due to the fact that Akasha resides within the sun sphere and Metatron will simply "swallow" his rival. However, as I mentioned before, this knowledge is inconsequential to present day humanity. I learned about the facts of Pluto's function by viewing it in the mental sphere. I am not allowed to divulge anything more at this point.

4.

The Peculiarities of the Higher Astral Planes

A student of the hermetic sciences knows that each zone or sphere possesses its own particular laws and ways. However, there are some noteworthy peculiarities found in the more subtle levels of the astral sphere that the hermeticist should be aware of.

In the material world, some people are affected by depression and other maladies that weigh heavily upon the human spirit in many ways. In the higher levels of the astral sphere, the opposite conditions prevail, that is to say that all individuals exist there in a state of constant elation. As a result, only immortal astral beings are able to abide on such higher planes of existence. The prevailing powerful oscillations would destroy a common or lesser astral being in an instant.

The higher astral world, also called "light-world", may be compared to the Mercury sphere, because the mental body has achieved divine elevations and all inhabitants of these lofty spheres have attained an utmost brilliance and genius. Astral physicians in this sphere frequently travel to lower astral levels to work in places of healing. Some astral beings, who have suffered difficult deaths, and thus carry their traumas into the astral sphere become patients in such places of healing in the astral sphere. Heavily traumatized individuals are people, who were murdered or died violently and therefore relive their traumas in the astral sphere due to the easy manifestation of imagination in the astral sphere. This way, the unfortunate victim will die the same way again and again.

Similarly, severe psychiatric diseases such as bi-polar disorders, clinical depression, compulsive-obsessive disorders, schizophrenia, etc. are inflictions that do not end at the moment of death, and specialists from the higher realms are sought to help these groups of individuals to overcome their obstacles and traumata.

Bodies of water are found in the higher realms, which can be used like a medium to see the most abstract occurrences of the universe, since no one here is interested in earthly matters anymore. Larger bodies of water, such as large lakes or oceans, are made of pure concentrated life force, in which the inhabitants may bathe. As a result, the bather develops more sensibility towards the elated life in this higher sphere.

On land, there are magnificent temple systems that immediately evoke a feeling of divine unity in the individual who visits these temples. Naturally, due to the abstract nature of ideals, there is an absence of diversity of confessions. Merely individual preferences to certain Gods may constitute of individuality of confessions.

Naturally, disease and disharmony do not exist in the high regions of the astral sphere. Surprisingly, animals and plant life are also found in the higher reaches of the astral world. However, these animals, trees and other plants consist of the principal group-souls of all species of animal and plant life forms. Therefore the animals here are highly developed and have their rightful place in the lofty regions of the astral sphere.

In addition to highly developed souls, there are un-incarnated human beings that are suspended in an unconscious dream-state. These humans need the oscillations of the high sphere to develop fertile ground for the divine seed to germinate when they mature through their various incarnations.

These sleepers are supervised by dream genii, which imprint some form of consciousness into the dreamer's mind, since un-incarnated humans lack an individual consciousness as they are transported from the mental sphere to the astral sphere.

An animal group-soul development progresses contradictory to the dreaming never-incarnated sleeper humans. From their present location, animal-group souls move in the mental sphere, where they transform to a tetra-polar magnet (human), only to return as non-incarnated sleeper humans back to the astral realm.

Due to the subtle and high oscillations that prevail in the high regions of the astral sphere, evergreen trees and plants in the elevated astral regions will be allowed to incarnate as new animal species. However, these processes are part of the preliminary spiritual preparation for the next Brahma Day on earth. During the evolutionary cycle of the next Brahma Day, humans, animas and plants of an entirely different character, shape and appearance will inhabit our earth.

Some of the main activities of the inhabitants of these elevated regions consist of the study of cosmic philosophy, Quabbalah and working with lower regions to enhance quality of oscillations in lower astral regions in accordance with evolutionary guidelines. Every human being here is acting creatively and hence attracts lofty mental ideas to the astral level so that they may be brought to fruition within the astral region.

5.

Shiva, the God of Destruction

The Godhead Shiva may be evoked by some of the ancient Indian mantrams. Some branches of Hinduism all over India and other places where this religion is practiced worship and venerate Siva. As a superior genius, he does not have to incarnate since he is not considered human.

As a patron of Yoga and Kundalini, Siva's true name is INDRA, the God of destruction. To be precise, Indra does not destroy anything on earth, or does he annihilate human beings; rather he destroys maya, ignorance, imbalance and disharmony. As a tetra-polar Godhead, Indra can be subdivided into Shiva (Indra) and Shakti, whereas Shakti represents the passive elements.

This glorious Godhead plays an important role in Karma and evolution within the entire macrocosmic creation. It is quite a task for even the most creative, spiritual master to put the attributes (id est, the Godhead in its entirety) into a mantric formula. Only through the separation of the Indra-Shakti entity are human minds capable of getting a glimpse of the constitution of this great primal being.

Spiritually, Indra's rank rivals that of a creator God

(Elohim). As one of the Gods that demonstrate great sympathy and compassion towards humankind, his countenance radiates might, love, omniscience and omnipresence. Indra's appearance symbolizes his royal rank in the heavenly world, donning robes of gold and a crown upon his brow. His body is well formed in ideal proportions. His true signature is similar to the AUM with some deviations.

Shiva displays a friendly and forthcoming demeanor, although the intense radiance of his divine aura may tax an ordinary human's consciousness. Hence, the sphere magus would be well advised to use a proper mantram to adjust his mental body to comfortably withstand Indra's radiance. Without the proper preparations, the magus will fall into an almost dimensionless state of relativity.

During my first encounter with this God, space began to dilate and again contract. I found myself in lofty heights in one instant only to hover almost at ground level the next moment. Those experiences and other peculiarities influenced my mind and body long after this encounter. Thus are the effects of Indra's mind-bending oscillations. They taught me just how relative existence can be. Indra reigns supreme in all spheres as he personifies one of the modifications of Akasha.

All three planes (material. Astral and mental) are within his sphere of influence. Indra can be regarded as the supreme authority of Kundalini Yoga. However, only advanced yogis are in a position to contact Indra in relation to this yogic art.

Within the lower coarser spheres of influence, Indra's may grant wishes or impact material endeavors favorably, which displays his compassion towards mankind. However, in higher aspects, his grandness and complexity may prove incomprehensible even for a high initiate.

Indra resides in a constant state of motion. Wherever he annihilates deceit, he immediately fills the void with cosmic universal truth. Owing to his nature, it is quite understandable, that through Indra's influence and guidance, Franz Bardon's hermetic works found their way to our material world within our times and not, as planned, in 500-600 years in the future.

Divine Providence considers Indra as a visible counterpart to itself. In the cosmic hierarchy, Indra is part of the mightiest and grandest of Godheads. His rank places him well above Brahma the creator God as well as Vishnu the creator-conservator. Ultimately, all three are one."

Upon the conclusion of this Brahma day in the far distant future, Indra will initiate the destruction of matter.

There are myriad of aspects that constitute this wonderful Godhead and no sphere magus should omit a contact with Indra.

6.

The Godhead of Christ

This is just not my place to make corrections to the New Testament of the bible. However, I will highlight other interesting aspects of this Godhead.

Christ was a fellow of the Brethren of Light, among the twelve elders. He descended to earth with the mission to teach a higher form of love that would reach beyond pure sexuality and tribal loyalty. Every individual on this planet will acquire true love through a substance that the Godhead of Christ bestowed upon the world and humankind. Once this substance comes to full fruition in humankind, no more major wars will plague the world, and self-destructive human tendencies will be substituted for a firm faith.

Due to Christ's great sacrifice, more individuals will develop tendencies toward the hermetic sciences. We all should thank this great Godhead for delivering us from self-destruction.

Upon his physical death on the cross, Christ remained in his astral form on this planet by his ability of densification of the earth element of in his astral form to attain a physical appearance in order to conclude his mission here on earth.

Once he left the physical realm behind, he realized in the astral sphere that his mental dissolution (into the divine light) became eminent. However, since Christ, an absolute and supreme being, who demonstrated his divine spirit through saving humankind from annihilation, he recreated his own self astrally and subjoined his unique self to his recreated astral form through a strong mental bond. In other words, he had cast his entire essence and personality inside the astral vessel, before he became one with Akasha or Nirvana. With this act, Christ will once more be able to descend to earth in time. Then he will have the high mission to personally guide and educate all those hermetic students, who have chosen Christ as their Godhead.

For this reason, a hermeticist, who has chosen the Godhead of Christ as his personal God, shall eventually experience Christ in all his grandeur, once the adept has learned the skill of unification with a Godhead.

Before his last incarnation and mission, Christ mastered all our known spheres in the hierarchy as well as 40 exomacrocosmic realms that lay beyond our macrocosmos. Later, he visited our sun's sphere frequently to cast the Quabbalistic ten-fold key, in order to gain influence onto the entire micro and macrocosmos and all the spheres contained within.

Christ often sought the company of Metatron, who bestowed upon Christ many unfathomable abilities. From within the sun sphere, Christ had the opportunity to visit the suns of hundreds of stellar systems. There he learned about different laws that are not identical to our system. In finding that Metatron is the source of all galactic solar systems, Christ mastered all the diverse modifications of Akasha and found enlightenment in all the extra-solar spheres.

Christ must receive our awe and utmost respect. He descended from the heights of existence down to our grizzly earth planet to experience disgrace, torture and execution on the cross just for the love of humankind. It must be stated that in Christ, a hermetic adept will see an image of Metatron.

7.

The Personal and Universal God

The supreme principle that we know is the Metatron principle. This is the absolute being, the conceptual "front face side" of God. Due to our limited capacities, the "far side" of God is the lack of being and existence; hence it is incomprehensible. Only a Godhead may know this nonbeing, non-existing Divine Providence. In human cultures, past and present, this side of Divine Providence has many names like God the Father, Allah, Shiva or Nirvana-Buddha, just to name a few. Although God may be worshipped differently and with different names, all cultures are basically worshipping one and the same supreme being.

At this point, the question may arise just why Christ said: "I am the right way, the truth, and the life. No one can come to the Father except through me." The same holds true in other faiths. For example, a Buddhist will strive to become a Buddha. Herein lies the secret of the personal Godhead. Through a personal Godhead, the practicing adept will advance towards as universal God. Once the adept assumes conscious unification with a personal Godhead, he or she will be enabled to easily communicate with other divine beings. In the Mercury sphere, all of its 144 genii are divine beings and not only there. I mentioned the Mercury sphere, because Quabbalah corroborates this fact. Only the divine will communicate with the divine and that is the law. This may serve as an example: If the adept wants to be noticed in the fire sphere, he must assume the form of a salamander. The same principle applies here.

For the advancing adept, a personal God constitutes the highest of all principles and nothing shall stand above. This attitude supplies the adept with the potency and wisdom to ascend to equal standing with other divine beings and communicate with them. An undeveloped spirit will not comprehend the reason of this universal law and its implications. Once chosen, the adept will not change a personal Godhead throughout the entire path of initiation. This Godhead embodies the highest cosmic principle for the adept that will aid the seeker to advance towards Metatron to the point where this personal Godhead principle will become one with the universal principle of God; it is summed up by one of the Sanskrit Mahāvākyas: Tat Tvam Asi (That art thou).

From here onward, the adept evolves gradually into a cosmic force that cannot be fathomed by a common human mind. It would be an illusory undertaking for a neophyte or general devotee to directly worship Metatron without the necessary steps, because neophytes have not matured properly to comprehend the nature of the God they worship.

An adept knows the universal laws and his own

limitations. However, he knows his personal God and takes refuge in the knowledge that by connecting to his ideal, his personal God, the adept will be guided consciously towards his goal. In religion, the path stops here, but for the magus, the path begins in all earnest.

8.

The Guardian Spirit

There are two categories of guardian spirits. In the first category, there are genii, which have never incarnated physically and the second category consists of highly advanced human spirits. Average human beings are guided by the genii — or commonly called "guardian angels" — of the former category. On the other hand, a single advanced human spirit guides hermetic students individually throughout their development. These guardian spirits of the second category must possess a high rank within the spiritual hierarchy.

The guardian spirit will always be alert to his protégé's actions and protect the neophyte through intuition and inspiration. In certain life-threatening instances, the guardian spirit may intervene on a physical level, which requires the guardian spirit to possess advanced skills.

The guardian spirit accompanies his protégé throughout all incarnations. This constant connection and interaction leads to a special parent-child bond between protégé and guardian spirit. The hermeticist will develop great sympathy and love towards his guardian. Unfortunately, the protégé will lose memory of this relationship at birth.

Meeting the guardian spirit for the first time, the protégé will at once recognize his guardian spirit and mentor. Such encounter may be quite emotional and right away, the budding hermetic student will realize what his mentor-protector has done for him in the past and will do in the future. The protégé will never owe his mentor anything, but obedience and respect.

During mental travels and during extreme encounters, the guardian spirit may become his protégé's master mentor and perform further initiations that are detrimental to the student's development.

However, the protégé will not develop a dependency on his guardian, because meetings and encounters are sporadic and not constant. Furthermore, the pace of progress of the student will be at the guardian spirit's discretion.

The guardian spirit will remain at his protégé's side, until the protégé will begin exploring the sun sphere. This fact alone indicates the advanced standing of our guardian spirits.

In the beginning, a guardian spirit's emphasis is the character equipoise of his protégé. Sometimes it is necessary for the guardian to take stern actions. On other occasions, he may demonstrate clemency, love or humor and may appease karma. It all depends on the protégé's actions in life. Should the student lack conviction in introspective work, the guardian spirit may evoke calamity to teach his protégé through mishaps and misfortune. A guardian spirit's task does not only consist of protecting his protégé, but also to expedite the student's development. The student may look at his or her character traits and karma to develop an understanding of his or her guardian spirit's individuality.

Alas, there are occasions, where the guardian spirit must abandon his protégé due to his student's lack of application and strive to move ahead. In such case, the guardian will be called off his post by Divine Providence and will be compensated for his efforts. Naturally, the hermetic progress of the former protégé will be halted throughout that particular incarnation, since magic progress is impossible without a guardian spirit, just as cosmic laws dictate. Therefore, a true hermetic student will always treat others kindly, while practicing restraint and stringency in reference to his or her own character.

Initially, most individuals do not appreciate their guardian spirit, since they are ignorant of the guardian's importance. Sooner or later, due to the guardian's appeal, the protégé will develop an instinctive desire to connect with his or her guardian.

Many hermetic lodges or spiritual societies hold the preposterous notion that the guardian spirit in a part of the higher SELF. The higher SELF, as described in introspection, is the condition of unification with the Divine.

9.

Credence – Akasha

Nothing exists without Akasha, even nothingness could not be maintained. Everything in the universe carries the spark of Akasha deep within. Ordinary humans carry the spark inside, although they are ignorant of its existence. It so happens, that some individuals lose their orientation, because of lack of inner support. Some are convinced that they are without faith, regardless of the fact they clearly follow ideals and seek to realize them. Others mechanically perform a set of empty rituals of a particular culture and/or religion, into which they were born.

However, with the beginning hermeticist, the situation is quite different. Before the neophyte takes the first step on the path of initiation, he takes to a God that is all supreme. This God provides support for the practitioner. Often, he will receive inspiration and intuition from his divine source. The hermeticist worships his God to the point, where he emulates his God's virtues. While emulating his Godhead, the hermeticist feels the process of cultivating his soul. The degree of manifestation stands in direct proportion to the degree of equipoise. Akasha is formless and through the process of character refinement, it takes on form.

Once the adept has achieved equipoise of character, the Akasha principle within the elements will guide the adept onto further endeavors. This way, mistakes are avoided, since God is now the hermeticist's guide. However, such a state can be achieved through deep and severe humility. Every outbreak of egotism in word, deed and thought would prove counterproductive in contacting God. In general egotistic individuals place themselves before God by relying on their own opinion and values, which are relative and not constant as are the universal laws. A personal (egotistical) opinion is one-sided and imbalanced, if universal laws do not support and accompany the deeds, rituals or thoughts of an individual.

I have encountered such unfortunate people, who in their pedantic opinion placed themselves before God. They said to be wise beyond reproach. Alas, those people just demonstrated their ignorance and narcissistic character, since they believed that they need no God for guidance. I truly pity those fallen individuals. Universal law prohibits interference, because they have to realize their debacle of their own accord. Credence and humility are the tools to escape this quagmire of egotism; otherwise, they may fall into the abysmal depths of darkness. In the end, they cannot blame anyone but themselves.

Even in darkness, Akasha stands by those fallen individuals, ready for them to rekindle the divine spark within by showing signs of remorse, humility and acknowledgement of guilt. Thus is the process of finding a God that has never abandoned the fallen individuals. Deep meditation and contemplation are the tools of deliverance. "Know thyself!" That is the way to the light where we all desire to evolve onward to the higher regions of existence. We will be victorious through humility.

10.

Force or Potency – Fire

Omnipotence was the primary emanation of God. Naturally, an ordinary human being subsists in a state of perpetual impotence. On the other hand, a practitioner, who practices the steps of the First Tarot Card, cultivates an increasing amount of fiery force that ultimately expresses itself in formidable willpower. On the path of initiation, the adept will need superhuman willpower to successfully ascend into higher levels and become the master of the elements and maintain absolute authority.

Such augmented willpower also benefits the adept in mundane life-situations. Force or willpower is the best tool to master life and master whatever fate holds in store for the adept. An individual, provided with a prominent amount of willpower will seemingly develop a stoic immunity towards life's many adverse situations. Consequently, the fire element will always accompany and guard the adept.

However, like everything else in our cosmos, power or force has two sides. Any individual, who uses his or her willpower for egotistical purposes, will inevitably decline in the end. In other words, Akasha will become the ultimate judge such an individual and will pass punishment accordingly.

Throughout history, strong willed individuals have misused their gift of willpower and ultimately, power was used negatively and destructively. Although, an adept may utilize the fire element from time to time in a destructive manner, when his mission dictates such use to correct imbalance, he will not abuse his authority for purely personal gain and will always proceed responsibly.

In Franz Bardon's step-by-step course in *Initiation into Hermetics*, the student will first learn to adequately master fire before moving on to master the remaining three elements. The fire principle's character is subtleness and yet power and force. The adept should always use caution: fire is hot and inherently dangerous if handled improperly. Simply put, wave your hand through the air, or hold it under water or dig in the ground, and chances are that no harm will come to you. But hold your hand into the flames of a fire and the consequences will be very unpleasant..

In essence, fire possesses the attributes of expansiveness and the radiation of the electric fluid. The adept will work with this fluid to heal the severest of ailments. The fire element is initially stored within Akasha and only upon exiting Akasha, the fire element will acquire its characteristics. Ultimately, fire the one element that is closest to Akasha, hence the adept will utilize this element to animate the other three elements. Moreover, the spawning principle produces the manifested faith. The neophyte is introduced to the fire element for the first time in Step III of Initiation into Hermetics. In this step, the neophyte utilizes pure imagination. However, once the student has reached Step V or VI, he or she will have developed the ability to invoke as well as evoke the fire element. As a matter of fact, it is this level, where true manipulation of fire occurs, without relying on imagination alone. The same applies to working with the other elements, whereby it should be noted that the air element proves to be the most difficult one to evoke. Simply put, imagination work will develop into a measurable reality and this reality must accordingly be in harmony with Akasha.

Due to its character of being the subtlest element, fire can be evoked more easily, when compared to the others. However, the difficulty to control this element demands a well-developed willpower, since fire's character is expansive, volatile, fleeting and etherical.

Owing to this elemental characteristic, alchemist will place great importance in controlling the fire element, which demands willpower coupled with attention to detail. For this reason, the basic tenet for the alchemist should be: no success without fire.

The highest aspects concealed within the fire element are the creator's all-might and omnipotence. God created the fire element by utilizing the Quabbalistic formula "SCH" (Engl. "sh" as in "she") and "K", hereby expressing fire's qualities and quantities on the highest level. Macrocosmically, the two Quabbalistic letters caused the so-called "big bang" and hence, the expansion of our universe from nothingness to existence of energy, matter space and the universal laws.

A human being — the microcosmos — also contains the all-might and omnipotence principle hidden away inside his or her Akasha principle. Ultimately, any individual holds the latent potential to develop these highest abstract virtues, commencing with simple will and gradually ascending up to the highest virtues of the fire element. All-might and omnipotence exist latently within the microcosm until unification with Godhead and thereby with Metatron. Only then, a human being shall transform into a macrocosmic being. Such a human Godhead has all the elemental forces at his or her disposal.

11.

Wisdom – Air

True wisdom may elude most present-day human minds. Sadly, the majority of humankind acts vacuously and dimwittedly. In addition, even educated individuals, who nurture knowledge and learned information alone, are schooled unilaterally. Alas, these problems even take place among the hermetic neophytes.

In the first place, air acts as a mediator. On one side, it receives the heat of fire, and on the other side air receives the coolness of water. In the interface between these two forces, wisdom is born. In other words, there were willpower and sentience (feeling) intercept, wisdom will result because the process of electric and magnetic interaction. Due to the subtle nature of air, this passive electromagnetic fluid can only exist within the air element, and unlike the characteristically bonding effect of the earth element, the fluids are unattached in the air element.

For this reason, the ancient cultures of the Hebrews and Egyptians deified the air element and an entire major Arcanum, the Fourth Tarot Card, was dedicated to the air principle. In this Arcanum, a whole path of initiation hinges upon this principle of wisdom. This fact emphasizes, that wisdom is not a pure virtue of water alone. The air principle alone does not epitomize perfection. However, the fact that fire and water reside within air latently, enables the air principle (together with fire and water exchanging within air) to be addressed by a major Arcanum.

Cosmically, the air element suggests the harmonizing and balancing principle. Its role is that of a mediator of water and fire. Only this balancing act provides persistence to the universe. As a matter of fact, the alchemist may create the Red Lion through this balancing principle. God utilized the Quabbalistic letter "A" (Engl. "aa" as in "aardvark") to create the air principle.

Moreover, wisdom does not manifest itself inside the cranium (brain), but in the solar plexus. Whenever wisdom manifests itself, the brain will fall silent. Only in the case of the clarification — explanation; communicating wisdom to others — of abstract concepts of wisdom, the adept guides the fluids into the head. During this process, however, the adept should be very attentive not to pollute wisdom with his or her own individual thought processes, so that wisdom does not degrade to mere knowledge. Only a well-balanced adept, whose fire and water elements are in equipoise, will be able to maintain pure wisdom. Hence, only highly evolved individuals exhibit the sign of genuine wisdom.

Every student of the hermetic path had been given

a portion of wisdom at birth. However, it is the student's responsibility to increase wisdom or lose it altogether. A word of warning: the loss of one's innate wisdom may end the path into initiation.

During the Akashic act of creation, the proto-elements first manifested themselves and out of those, the four cosmic elements that constitute our universe are generated. The process cannot be explained, because creation is based upon the Quabbalistic ten-fold key, a concept that is still unfathomable at this time of our human evolution.

12.

Love – Water

Only a few privileged individuals perceive true love, experience its depth and are conscious of his or her blessings.

Love is the one aspect, which favors the alleviation of karma. Naturally, hate poses the opposite aspect that results in accruement of Karma. Once a hermeticist has reached divine love, hate must be eradicated on all levels. Love is patient, forgiving, respectful, eternal and tolerant. It is the sympathy towards all humans and spirit beings. Only adepts, who develop this level of human love, will obtain hermetic love, a level of love that allows an individual to endure any negative karma.

Love is the second commandment of God. Anyone ignorant of this truth should cast aside any hermetic ambitions. God is eternally generous and his leniency is without bounds. Only WILL stands above love and influences this Divine aspect and lends love greater value.

We commit our deepest love towards our children. They are innocent before God and no one ought to punish children harshly and with malcontent or hatred. Child abuse is a crime against God. A child stands under the care of God and maltreatment of a child will evoke the ominous dark clouds of karma.

Any human being that feels loved will flourish through love, convalesce when sick and heals emotional wounds quicker. Thus are the lower levels of the laws of love that any common individual should be aware of, in order to live harmoniously among fellow human beings, lest he or she wishes to sow sorrow and misery. An adept, who ignores the laws of love, will be inflicted with disease, the realization of the hermetic path will be frustrated and Maya will cloud the adept's judgement. The consequences are as follows: No more success with the exercises and introspection; an attack upon faith, being overwhelmed and profound self-dissatisfaction and hatred. All this will ultimately lead towards hate towards certain objects of affection, systems or persons.

The most profound variant of hate consists of the withdrawal of love and affection. All students of the hermetics should think twice about the treatment of fellow humans. Every action warrants a reaction. Divine Providence will reward us accordingly. The fairy tale of Mother Hulda (Frau Holle) and the kind and unkind girl serves a good example.

The adept compares fellow humans to children and will treat each one with respect and love. Of course, an adept directs his or her highest love to his Godhead. After all, love is the law. A human being hates others, consequently only hates his or her own self. Love is so pure, that a person may not even take notice. They may be paid passively in form of instructions and guidance. These are the gifts that the adept may bestow upon fellow humans, children and adults alike.

An adept wishes to imitate his or her own Godhead and its eternal undying love. Such a Godhead comes in many forms such as Christ, Maha-Devi, Krishna or Indra. For all beings, love is cherished as the highest treasure. Consequently, God will turn away from anyone, whose actions are inhumane.

Thus is the law of love.

13.

Consciousness – Earth

The consciousness is retained by the interactions of the three elements. Although all human beings have a consciousness, the average individual dwells in a semi-conscious state of existence. Detrimental strokes of fate jolt the consciousness of the afflicted individual. It is the aim of karma's to awaken all humankind into full consciousness. Through the use of the faculty of consciousness, our true EGO, an awakened individual may control and evaluate all thoughts, before they enter the mental matrix. This way the adept will be able to make the decision, whether to allow the thought to pass through or reject a thought altogether (see Step I, Magic Mental Training, Initiation into Hermetics).

The EGO is a tetragrammaton and our mental body is therefore the image of God. In order to realize consciousness of the mental body, a neophyte adept schools all four astral elements. Once the student reaches an equipoise of the soul mirror, he or she will be able to influence the mental body through the mental matrix and the physical body through the astral matrix. The astral component presents the mediator that reflects into the mental as well as the physical. As a result, the adept will also fortify Akasha, which results in the refinement of the entire human being and its three bodies through via its matrices.

On the material level, everything is tetra-polar. The "four-poled" magnet gives matter coherence. Without it, the universe would simply fall apart.

Through the EGO, the practitioner will perceive and guide the spiritual body in its entirety. Additionally, the practitioner must be perfecting the EGO. The Divine aspect of EGO is omni-consciousness or omnipresence, a virtue that the adept will realize through his or her step by step, commencing with thought vacancy, as Franz Bardon describes it. A practitioner who reaches a certain depth of though vacancy will eventually perceive omnipresence. For this reason, Bardon advises the adept to keep practicing and deepening thought vacancy throughout the course of Initiation into Hermetics..

In Step X of Initiation into Hermetics, the adept is mandated to imagine omnipresence. Apparently, there is a relationship between thought vacancy and this step. The nature of the untrained human mind prohibits proper imagination of something that has not previously been seen before. Hence, the adept who is working the exercises of this step will have achieved a certain depth of thought vacancy and proficiently remains in the state of vacancy successfully for one to two hours. Through intense vacancy of thoughts over lengthy periods of time, the adept will reach a certain point, where this omnipresence will reveal itself. The adept will reach omnipresence by exercising the mind with a simple thought vacancy exercise in the first step to ultimately reach the Godhead itself in the last step.

I personally have perceived this manifestation of Akasha in the form of pure credence. At that time, I concluded that God accompanied me on my path, although I was not in a position to consciously perceive this God initially. Once I achieved Divine unification, I fully understood the concept of omnipresence. The adept will learn to assume this form of consciousness at will or abstain from it.. This experience will leave a great impression that will properly guide the adept, even while operating through the normal consciousness.

14.

Introspection: Yes or no?

It is a misconception that after years of practicing introspection, an individual will become virtuous and develop great attributes that differentiate such an individual from the masses. However, my observations show that this not the case. The average person has a certain set of attributes in accordance with his or her evolutionary development and often one may find an average individual with a virtuous radiance. Some of these average individuals have even achieved equipoise of character, although they may have never heard anything about magic, hermetics or mysticism. What place does the hermetic practitioner take, whose aim is attain noble character and seek advanced spiritual knowledge and wisdom through the science of all sciences? On the positive side, the hermeticist may have been able to ennoble some aspects of his or her character through hard work In the light of these observations, I drew the following conclusion: One must first become an ethical human, before one considers becoming a hermeticist.

A neophyte practitioner is not at liberty looking down on his or her fellow humans. In many cases, a neophyte's character is not any nobler than that of others, with whom we interact daily. Every action begins as a thought. Thought control and thought composure and discipline are our first steps towards adepthood. Those exercises enable the practitioner to dispel any forthcoming thought that is deemed incongruous to our training. At the beginning of our training, we have constructed a soul mirror to show us our positive and negative attributes. Through diligent thought training, we have an opportunity to stifle unwanted thoughts that may lead to misdeeds or entice us to nurture negative attribute in our character.

We should be looking into our souls daily, so that we will not hurt others or ourselves. I dealt with this subject in my little book, A Practice Guide. Regardless of the fact that everyone can read, only the few understand. Read between the lines; take a closer look inside yourself! My spirit recognizes destructive and constructive thought forms and controls both through the superior "element" of faith. For this reason, that all practitioners should work this way, so that they would see success in their exercises. This is how I worked and succeeded, and I am convinced that no one would lament the excessive difficulty of the hermetic path anymore. Remember: upon your death, you will be called upon what you did with the gift that Divine Providence has bestowed upon you at birth. Should you then answer that it was too difficult to handle, or you did not understand what to do? Indeed not. How foolish would we "hermetic magi" appear at the threshold on the astral plane? Our ultimate goal should be initiation and not decadence or squander of life forces. It is not my intention to insult or hurt the practitioner, but rather nudge him or her in the right path and the proper attitude. For this reason, the practitioner should amass courage and faith along the way. The one, who treads the path, is a chosen one, who reaches far beyond the mediocrity of the masses. God gave you dignity, so use it. Those harsh words are meant to spark the inner divine fire.

15.

True Rune-Magick

This field of magick sciences is considered less demanding when compared to other systems within this field and its lurking dangers are unsurpassed as well. Although, rune-magick is linked to Quabbalah, it is not identical to the system of Franz Bardon's work, *The Key to True Quabbalah*. True to our cosmic system of duality, every rune has an opposing negative rune aspect or anti-rune, if you will.

The following example should emphasize the true danger of this system: Should the rune-magus speak a rune that symbolizes love through the three senses (like Quabbalistic letters), he must have evaluated his character that no traces of the opposing trait to love, namely hate, still lingers deep and unnoticed within his soul. He must be convinced without doubt that no shadow, no matter how miniscule, may cloud the pure virtue of love within the magus. A key characteristic of a rune is the fact that its power, once evoked by the rune-magus lingers even after its magical use and while the magus performs mundane tasks. Incidentally, the guardian of the evoked rune resides near the magus for some time after the evocation proper to uphold the force that the rune contains, and for demonstrative purposes, should a person of misgivings cross the rune practitioner's path and a brief, almost unnoticed feeling of dislike (hate) awakens within the magus, the rune's polarity is reversed instant and the guardian of hate (everything in the universe has two sides) takes control of the rune. Only a well-schooled rune-magus acknowledges the change in its early stages to take the opportunity to end the negative rune's reign.

However, a mediocre rune-magus will not notice this exchange until the subject of dislike or hatred has been afflicted by great misfortune, emotional and physical maladies or even death. The rune-magus will register a drastic elevation of hate inside, which involuntarily projects against the subject of hate and the point of reversing the causes had long been surpassed. Now the magus is involuntarily working and dealing with the anti-rune and had become the pawn of the negative forces. Considerable damage has been done. The demon has found a victim. Since all the karmic responsibilities of the results of demonic activities are solely placed on account of the rune magus.

Sooner or later, a judge of the Saturn sphere will evaluate the deeds of the rune-magus to see if his conscious mind and willpower enable him to halt his evil way. That way, the level of punishment may become less severe. However, should the magus ignore his consciousness and continue his ways, the judge will hold court and mete out severe punishment. The former magus – although he cannot be called a magus henceforth – finds himself struck gravely in a never-ending series of misfortunes and the heaviest of karmic implications. His guardian spirit abandons him in time of dire needs, and this wretched soul is left to his own devices. Ultimately, the former magus is thrust into the depth of darkness, woe and abasement, well beyond the scope of the average miscreant.

This wretched subhuman creature that this former rune-magus has become, has been cursed to live below any basic dignity of even the lowest of human existences. It may take 10 incarnations of more to enjoy life again as an average human being, let alone become a practicing magus once again. His development had been frozen for centuries to come and he may wish he never dabbled in this form of magick in the beginning.

A true rune-magus, who is a hermetic practitioner that has reached true equipoise, may find rune-magick of great value in his development, since it could ease the path of adepthood. The true magus will apply the powers of the runes for the greater good of humankind. He may even help himself, if the need arises. A magus of noble character, however, will not take advantage of the powers due to his humility before God, but devote his powers to the good of his fellow humans. Just like our Master Bardon, who did use his great powers for personal gains.

The above example should serve as a warning to the casual dabbler of rune-magick. By applying great caution, a truly balanced hermetic practitioner, may proceed and harvest the fruits that the practice of rune-magick may bear. In a previous incarnation, I almost doomed myself through the rune practice. Intuition and foresight prevented an oncoming disaster. I paid restitution to avert a personal catastrophe and aided the person wronged by my use of rune-magick in any way possible. In the end, I succeeded in the reversal of the negative oscillations of the rune.

Presently, I am writing a book on the rune knowledge I gathered in this previous life. In this book, I plan to reveal knowledge that has been lost over time. Alchemists will greatly profit from that knowledge, since there are runes that can be applied to alchemical processes.

16.

Ufology

Around the world, people are talking about the existence or non-existence of UFOs. An adept will know that there are intelligent life forms in the physical universe aside our planet earth. There are billions of possibilities of intelligent existence in the billions of galaxies. However, a close look at the physical universe and the great distances that separate the objects in space, will make an observer realize that space travel to distant stars or galaxies is physically impossible. Even our closest neighboring star system, Alpha Centauri is at a distance of 4.3ly. It would take even an advanced space ship thousands of years to reach this Alpha Centauri. Light travels at 671 million mph or 1080 million km/h and mass cannot travel at this speed, as it would require infinite energy to maintain this velocity.

Despite this limitation, there are UFO sightings all over the world. About 90% are false sightings. So there are 10% of real sightings. How are UFOs able to travel to our earth? How do they overcome the vast distances? Many exoplanets harbor advanced civilizations. Most civilizations, for example, in the Milky Way galaxy, are more advanced than our own.

Among these civilizations, there are advanced magi, who

utilize their life force to shield their mental bodies during intergalactic travel. This way they mental travel outside the space/time continuum and bridge many million light years instantly. Sometimes, these aliens also mental travel in groups.

Most of these alien adepts are invisible to the naked eye. However, sometimes they may become visible or rather their life force "space ship" will be seen doing incredible feats that seem physically impossible to the observer as their life force hull may pick up some of the denser elements of the lower parts of the astral sphere. These "ships" are made of life force and travel without physical restrictions. Therefore, travelling aliens do not have to consider physical speed constraints, nor limits due to gravitation or centrifugal forces. For this reason, some UFOs are seen accelerating at fantastic speeds, performing backbreaking acrobatics across the skies or skip 10 miles or more in an instant.

These alien beings also land on the surface from time to time for the purpose of researching our earth. However, contact is limited to earthling adepts, due to the fact that these aliens are visiting with their mental bodies and if they wish for contacts they are required — similar to earth adepts' visits to element beings — to mimic our mental shape to become visible to earth adepts. Since the mental language is universal to all spiritual beings, communication would be quite possible. This way, they will learn about our civilizations, past and present.

Indeed, initiates from many intelligent races, from all corners of the universe, visited and are visiting our planet. After all, the process is the same for all beings. The virtues of morality and immorality exist throughout the universe and, as always, Akasha will keep checks and balances, so that no chaos engulfs our evolution. The cosmic travelers, who are of great moral standing, will naturally adhere to the cosmic laws, so that no harm will come to them or the earthlings.

On most planets that harbor life, evolution stands at a much more advanced level, opposed to to our planet. A conversation with an alien traveler can be quite captivating, although the complexity of their cultures and laws may appear quite abstract for our minds to conceptualize. However, all life in the universe is bound to the same divine laws. Extraterrestrial beings only travel with their mental body in a vessel of life force, while their physical and astral bodies remain on their home planet. Hence their bodies are invisible to the untrained physical eye.

As noted above, light travels at 186282.39 mps (299792458 km/s). Light speed is the oscillation, where all material dissolves. Objects that have mass can approximate this limit, but cannot travel at this speed or beyond, so that prevents material matter becoming astral. That is a universal cosmic law and all beings in the material universe have to adhere to this law. For this reason, material space travel over light year distances would prove impossible.

This concise treatise should shed some light on extraterrestrial visits and the UFO phenomena. Among our human population, there are highly advanced beings, such as Franz Bardon, who have travelled to other solar systems and conversed with initiates within extraterrestrial populations, in order to gather useful wisdom.

17.

Time and Eternity

We know time as past, present and future*. Most individuals dwell in the past and revive old events, whether they are positive or negative and by the same token, these individuals also dwell mentally in the future, extensively planning out future events. The presence stands between past and future. Present tense is the equivalence of elimination of time. Living in the NOW, the adept effectuates present tense. The past tense disappears and the future blends together with the presence, the NOW. Living in the NOW, is the same as being immortal or eternal. Even when our body demises, our NOW-consciousness lives on eternally.

Consciousness is mind or spirit and unites all the elements. The spirit is the image of God and therefore it is immortal. Nothing should inhibit us to live in the NOW. Only an imbalanced soul subjugates our consciousness to the time phenomenon. Even a relatively balanced student should be able to maintain the state of the NOW. The adept will naturally draw on past experiences and events to employ them as tools that are necessary to aid in present time events. In reference to the future, the adept will make preliminary plans.

Through discipline and training, the student will ease into this NOW-state-of-mind, which will become second nature to the trained adept. This state can be experienced, but not described. This is a state of Akasha. An individual, who lives in the NOW will make great strides, mystically and magically, because the consciousness manifests credence. Even the hardest exercises and problems are then solved with comparative ease.

18.

*Past, Present and Future

By Peter Windsheimer

"Neither is there a smallest part of what is small, but there is always a smaller (for it is impossible that what is should cease to be). Likewise there is always something larger than what is large."

Amaxagoras (500BC-428BC)

God made a universe that is able to make itself

Teilhard de Chardin

Traditionally, humankind separates time into past, present and future. A future event that comes into fruition is considered a present event and once the event concludes, it becomes a past event. However, upon close observation, we realize that there is no present event in the time-space continuum. The only conditions that can be monitored by a rhythmic device are the past and present events. Although we can materially only know the existence of the past as reality does not render the future non-existent. Since we are physically bound to time and space continuance, we have no conscious perception of future events until they become a past event. However, that fact does not make it less real than past events. Basically past and future events do not physically exist altogether, regardless of the fact that we have memories of perceiving future events in becoming past events through our consciousness, which only exists in the present tense. One could argue that the present tense is the only aspect of time and space that is real.

Even though, the presence or NOW does not exist physically, it is the one point that is perceived as real, however without containing space or time. The present tense does not contain time. Even a nanosecond ($10-9$ seconds) has a beginning and an end and while the nanosecond is passing, part of it lies in the past and the other part in the future. Therefore, the present tense is not within a time range. Just like the center of a rotating sphere. Mathematically, there is a center. However, this point is conceptual and therefore occupies no space. This point is the mere location of the center and since it is not an object, it contains neither space nor time. Hence it does not rotate with the sphere itself.

The German physicist and Nobel Price laureate, Max Planck, discovered what is called Planck Time, Planck Length and Planck Mass, the smallest units for anything physical to occur. Plank length is $1.6 \times 10-35$ meters (the United States uses a decimal point instead of a decimal comma). That is the smallest physically measurable unit that lends validity to time, space and gravity. Planck Length coincides with Plank Time. Planck time, $5.39121 \times 10-44$ seconds, the smallest quantum that gives causality in our universe validity. Consequently, the cause and effect phenomenon occupies time and space, however small those quanta may be. We can see that we won't be able to tackle the phenomenon of present tense on a physical level. In our physical universe, cause and effect cannot take place simultaneously. Cause and effect are separated by a time-like interval that moves from the future to the past without a clear separation of present tense. Technically, we cannot determine, where the cause stops and the effect takes place; they blend together like the colors of the sky at sunset.

The cosmic speed limit is 299,792.458 meters per second. This limit is reserved for phenomena that are without mass (Photons are energy particles). Anything beyond this speed would violate causality, since no effect can happen before the cause. A simple demonstration would be a signal or a message sent through space at twice the speed of light. The message would simply be received, before it was transmitted. Special relativity does not permit communication faster than the speed of light, without violating causality. Everything that exists is in motion and without a clear distinction of the concept of a physically present tense.

This is the place, where the concept of the NOW in the hermetic sense comes to play. According to Bardon, the Now is related to the Akasha principle. This principle exists, just like the present (NOW), without time and space. Akasha is basically "conceptless" or lacking any concept, relative to our physical senses and consciousness, our understanding and intellect. Its state is beyond existence of anything created and exists in our universe. As created beings, we cannot conceptualize the moment, the universe came into being (the big bang was not really a "bang" in the sense of a burst), because only a existing being could observe something existing or in the process of being created. However, there was nothing created, before creation to acknowledge the first step of creation. In this case, the cause that caused the first move in creation does not exist. It lies within the uncreated Akasha.

Pondering upon a prime cause is futile for our human minds. A created being cannot analyze that which is not. There is no electric or magnetic Akasha (positive and negative). Since the idea of Akasha cannot be understood with our minds — the created cannot understand the uncreated — our language dictates to circumscribe Akasha with familiar terms. Out of necessity, the first step of creation is the point, the beginning, which is in our case, present tense, a "moment" — so to speak — that is timeless and spaceless. I point that occupies no time and no space, but the concept of centrality. If we could remain in the true present tense, we would exist in a state of Akasha, without beginning and without end. Once our universe ceases to exist, including other spheres, it will be as if nothing ever existed. Then, our universe will be irrelevant, just as it was "before" existence. This is the reason, why our path shall be the one that embraces Akasha, become as the non-created. Otherwise, existence as we know it physically and spiritually, becomes without meaning.

Epilogue

by

Peter Windsheimer

Hopefully, the reader enjoyed the contents of this book. The first part is based on biographic material and the second part is a collection of treatises that were gained through experience.

I have personally known Seila Orienta and I can attest to his love for truth and his simple and yet effective ways of dealing with his students' problems along the path. I will always remember his generosity and selfless engagement to the cause.

Now, after his physical passing, it is up to the individual student to utilize all the gifts that he or she has received from Seila Orienta.

Peter H. Windsheimer

Epilogue

by

Johannes H. von Hohenstätten

It is a pleasure to be allowed to publish this autobiography of my dear friend and mentor, who dedicated it to his oldest son and student Daniel. I was privileged to reading the manuscript over 17 years ago and I am astonished about its content, every time I reread these pages.

The content of this work proves to be quite different, when compared to some of the other writings.

J.H. von Hohenstätten

Other Books Available at
Hermetic League Publishing

- **Seila Orienta:**

    The Golden Book of Wisdom

    Alchemy — The Mysteries of
    the Philosopher's Stone

    A Practice Guide

    The Hermetic Genesis

- **Johannes von Hohenstätten**

    The First Lesser Arcanum

Notes:

FSC
www.fsc.org

MIX

Papier aus ver-
antwortungsvollen
Quellen

Paper from
responsible sources

FSC® C105338